MEN ON WOMEN

MEN ON WOMEN

Jerry Gillies

DODD, MEAD & COMPANY
New York

Published by Dodd, Mead & Company, Inc.
79 Madison Avenue, New York, N.Y. 10016
Distributed in Canada by
McClelland and Stewart Limited, Toronto
Manufactured in the United States of America
First Edition

Library of Congress Cataloging in Publication Data

Gillies, Jerry, 1940–
  Men on women.

  1. Love. 2. Women. 3. Men. 4. Interpersonal relationships. I. Title.
HQ801.A5G54 1984   306.7   84-1498
ISBN 0-396-08281-5

CONTENTS

INTRODUCTION

This book project has been like a wonderful relationship with an exciting woman: consistently filled with delightful surprises. It's surprising that it got written at all, triggered as it was by a chance question, one woman asking another, "What in the world *do* men want from women?" I'm surprised at how close I feel to the men interviewed, surprised at how much I learned about what I want from women, and thoroughly surprised, as I think you will be, at some of the conclusions reached by the one hundred and one men involved in this exploration. And perhaps the biggest surprise of all is that no one had ever asked men these questions before.

You are about to read a biased book indeed, for this is

certainly not a broad-based statistical survey of what *all* men want from all women. It is, rather, a highly personalized survey by one man inviting very individualized comments from one hundred other men—one hundred loving, sensitive, willing-to-be-open-and-vulnerable men in all walks of life throughout the country, each of whom was personally recommended by at least one woman before being interviewed.

What do men really want from women? What attracts one man to one woman? What scares men most about women? What do sensitive men want women to be, do, and say? What does a man most want to tell a woman? All encounters between men and women would be much more fulfilling if the answers to these and dozens of other questions were clearly understood by both men and women. That is the purpose of this book: to ask the questions and get honest, open, and useful answers. The men who have responded to these questions have shared their deepest feelings, their fondest desires, their fears and disappointments—and often say things that might otherwise have remained unsaid their entire lives.

In conducting hundreds of workshops on relationships and writing several books on the subject, it's become apparent that one of the biggest obstacles to a successful relationship is the unchallenged assumptions brought to that relationship by both partners. This book challenges many of these assumptions.

The author isn't the only one surprised in this process. Many of the men interviewed reported that specific questions caught them off guard, forcing them to delve into areas of their emotional belief systems that had remained untouched. As one man put it, "[They] got me to reexamine what I *really* wanted from a woman, not just what I always *thought* I wanted." And *that* is one of the primary purposes of this book, to probe beyond the superficial wishes and desires expressed by men who are casually asked casual questions about one of the great issues in human experience: what men and women want from each other. Proving that some of the most wonderful truths are said in jest, our great national treasure, humorist and philosopher George Burns said, "The matter is simply that men and women want different things. Men want women, and women want men."

Men and women *do* want different things, do speak different languages. They are members of quite different biological and psychological species.

So then, what is the purpose of this book? It started out, quite simply, with one major focus: answering the question so many women ask so many times: "What *do* they want from us?" The varied and fascinating answers to the provocative questions that follow will certainly fill in a lot of the gaps for women who are interested in what men really want—particularly the men they say *they* want: the warm, sensitive kind of man who really likes, can honestly relate to, and openly communicates with women on a person-to-person basis. To be successful in any endeavor, and especially in creating and maintaining a happy love relationship, one must have a clear vision of what one wants and then be able to communicate that vision to the other person. In reading the responses to probing questions directed at men willing to be probed, women will get a clearer vision of what men want from them. This can also lead to a better understanding of what they want for themselves in a relationship, of what they are willing to give to men, and of how the two sexes might come together in mutually nourishing ways.

In addition to providing information about men to women, the book and the survey evolved to provide a powerful tool for men to learn more about themselves—more about what they want and more about what they don't want or need from women. A relationship is really a negotiation. As in any negotiation involving two people, each person has to know what he or she wants, whether it can be delivered by the other, whether he or she really wants it *from* the other, and whether he or she is willing to give the other person what *they* want in return.

Asking the Right Question

Another unanticipated facet of this book was that the questions would become just as important as the answers. I don't know why this should have surprised me. In my first book, *My Needs, Your Needs, Our Needs* (published in 1974 by Doubleday, Signet paperback still in print), a book designed to help couples communicate more effectively, I included one hundred questions for a man and woman to ask each other. As I wrote then, "Many of the problems in a relationship are due to the simple lack of information. When you don't know something about someone, you tend to fill in the vacuum with assumptions, fantasies, and unrealistic expectations. During the beginning of a relationship, we often are so wrapped up in the initial excitement that we fail to ask some very basic questions. These can be very simple "who" and "why" and "what" questions, or they can cover much broader areas of emotional response."

These one hundred questions ranged from "What was your favorite toy as a child?" to "Where would you like our relationship to be in a year?" and "What do you think you mean to me?" While this questionnaire was just a small segment of the book, it received by far the most comment and praise. Parts of it have been quoted in a number of other books through the years, and many psychologists and marriage and family counselors have told me how effective it's been in getting couples to share new and important information. When his book *Your Erroneous*

Zones was at the top of the bestseller list, Dr. Wayne Dyer looked me up to tell me that this questionnaire was one of the most powerful tools he had ever discovered in working with couples and training marriage counselors. Considering all these glowing comments, I've decided to include the love-partner questionnaire as a special appendix to this book.

It all comes to this: You can't get the answer if you don't ask the question. And the questions asked of the one hundred men who contributed to this project are even more deeply personal than those I created a decade ago. So another facet of this book is to use the questions themselves as a learning process. As you read through the book and come to individual questions, you might use them to learn more about yourself.

As a woman, you can ask yourself several questions about each of these questions:

- "Is this something I'd like to know about a man I'm interested in or involved with?"
- "How do I think most men would answer this question?"
- "How do I think a warm, loving, sensitive, vulnerable man would answer?"
- "How do I think a man I am specifically interested in would answer?"
- "How would I most like a man in my life to answer this question?"
- "If I were to ask myself a female version of this question, how would I answer it?"

And, as a man, you can ask yourself:

- "How do I answer this question?"
- "Is this a question I have ever asked myself before?"
- "Is my answer any different from the one I think a woman would want to hear?"

- "Can I identify with the selective group of men who responded to this survey?"
- "Knowing my answer to this question, how can I more effectively choose or relate to a relationship partner?"

A Personal Quest

Some of the responses to some of the questions are my own, for I have taken the survey along with my one hundred interviewees. These are questions I chose to ask myself in my personal quest for love in my life. And even some of *my* answers surprised me!

In 1972 and 1973, when I was writing *My Needs, Your Needs, Our Needs,* I thought I knew all there was to know about women, love, and relationships. So much new information and awareness has come to me in the intervening years, and I can now admit the surface has hardly been touched. Most of what I have learned in a life filled with much love has come from women, and because some very special women in my life were so much better at loving than I was, they became my teachers. Ten years ago, I wouldn't have thought to ask the questions in this book, let alone been able to answer them.

One of the most popular workshops I've ever conducted was a monthly series entitled The Love Lab, presented for several years in Miami. At these all-day sessions, men and women experimented with new behavior in the form of communication exercises, mainly revolving around telling each other what they wanted and then asking for it. A surprisingly large number of couples who met at these workshops entered highly successful long-term relationships. I suspect the reason for this phenomenon is simply that the discussions and games enabled those participating to communicate their wants at a deeper level than normal social interaction usually encourages. It's a lot easier to ask for what you want if you know exactly what it is, how and why you want it, who you want it from, and when you want it. And you stand a much greater chance of getting what you want if you know and understand what the other person wants. In sales training seminars I've conducted, a major point of attention is increasing the seller's awareness of what the buyer really wants. "Find out what they want and give it to them" is the credo of any successful sales/marketing effort. All relationships involve a kind of sales presentation, with the man and the woman alternating in the roles of buyer and seller.

Find Out What He Wants

One of the most sensitive and creative men I know, writer Ray Bradbury, once described the secret of writing a successful novel as simply finding out what your main character wants most in life and then letting them go after it. Just as simply, the way to have a happy relationship is to find out what your partner wants most out of the relationship and then to give it to them. In conversations with men, time and again they've told me that women often came into a relationship with a predetermined set of answers to questions they never got around to asking the man. Preconceived notions that are never checked out, never replaced with real answers, remain fantasy. And while fantasy may be the glue that holds together a relationship at its beginnings, only the mutual sharing of reality will allow it to expand with love and understanding.

What is the best way for a woman to attract a sensitive, caring man into her life? Find out what he wants and find a way to deliver it. In examining the hundreds of responses from such men on the following pages, we can get a clear idea of what most of them want most often. This preliminary information can then be checked out against actual information from a specific man.

What is the best way for a man to eliminate stress and confusion from his relationships with women? To clarify exactly what he wants and ask for it. The many varied questions contained herein can simplify the clarification process.

We humans are often very arrogant in thinking we know what will make us happy. The reason some of the questions probe so deeply beneath the surface is that our surface wants are quite often misleading, particularly when it comes to choosing love partners. We quite often choose the wrong person at the wrong time for the wrong reason. Freedom of choice, as wonderful as it is and as necessary to the human spirit, also means freedom to make dumb mistakes. It is no accident that earlier arranged marriages had a much better longevity record than current marriages do.

Many of the things we think we want are merely what we've been taught to want by our parents and important others in our lives. We can only really know what we want when we have examined it closely, experienced it, and found it produces the desired results. Many wants are fantasy wants. There's nothing wrong with that unless it gets in the way of reality. If I say that what will make me happy is a thirty-five year old woman with a beautiful figure and long, blond hair, and then a forty-five year old woman with short, dark hair gives me all I could dream of in nourishing, loving attention but I can't accept that because it doesn't meet my predetermined image of what I want, then I am sabotaging myself.

Choosing a Feeling

Rather than having rigid specifications in what I want from a woman, I have certain feelings I want to feel, certain physical and psychological sensations that give me pleasure. And I am deeply thankful that I've allowed myself to experience some wonderful feelings with wonderful people who were as far as can be imagined from what I thought I wanted.

We can never know it all. We can never know exactly what we want. Life is a process of discovering what it is that will make us feel fulfilled. In order to make room for these discoveries, we have to let go of our preconceived notions. It's a gradual unfolding process, one that lasts a lifetime. Part of the excitement of living and growing and learning is the continual uncovering of more of what we want for ourselves. There are things each of us want that we haven't begun to suspect yet. For the men who contributed so much to this project, as for me, answering these questions has sped up some of the unfolding process.

Part of the preparation for this book involved my attending and participating in a men's consciousness group in West Los Angeles. All of the men were highly creative, successful in their fields of endeavor, and struggling with the issues of male-female roles and relationships. We played around with a few of the questions that appear here. Each of the men found this uncovered so much in the way of thoughts and feelings that he was going to need a lot of time to think about it, to decide what to do with all this new emotional material and how it was going to affect his current relationship. One thing is certainly true: No man can ask himself all of these questions without changing himself, without becoming a different relationship partner.

I am not the same man I was before answering these questions. I can't say I know exactly how this will affect future relationships. If I had to quickly respond on this point, I would have to say that where I once had a list of things I wanted a woman to give me, I am now more willing to see *what* she gives me and *then* to decide whether I like it and want more of it.

Two Traumatic Events

The reason this book was written now—and the reason it's important for men to clarify their vision of what they want right now—is that we are all just beginning to recover from the two most traumatic events in human relationships: the sexual revolution and the women's liberation movement. We men haven't yet reassessed our wants on the basis of what we've learned from these two events. We are still holding on to what we thought we wanted under the old rules, when men were sexual, made *all* the moves and decisions, and women knew their place. Now women are sexual, make a lot of the moves and decisions, and we wish we knew *our* place. And all of this has happened in the past ten or twelve years!

If anyone had asked me what I wanted back in 1970, I never would have said that I want women to be as sexually forward as men or more independent, self-sufficient, and sure of themselves. And yet, I find myself much happier with the women of today than with the women of 1970. So I must be getting something good out of all this change, even though it's been confusing and sometimes painful to experience. All of this upheaval of old patterns and roles has created a situation in which we men are less sure of what we want than we were before—and sometimes less able to recognize it when we get it.

Another purpose in writing this book is to let women know that we men have been shocked to our very cores by all these changes, that we need all the help we can get in understanding what we really want. The man who says he hasn't been knocked off balance in the past decade hasn't been out there participating.

When men get together with other men to talk about themselves and women, and when they feel safe doing so, they reveal themselves as never before. This is the kind of revelation that comes across in many of the upcoming responses, the kind of sharing that heretofore men have only been willing to do with other men. One of the statements I made to the men answering the questions was, "Realize that here is a chance to be perfectly honest, to tell women what you want without fear of rejection. Remember, we serve women best when we tell them what we *really* want rather than what we think they want to hear."

In addition to quoting a few of the actual answers for each question, I have chosen to let you know why that particular question was included on my list. There's also an overview of the general consensus among these men for each area of questioning and for each specific question, along with my comments on the results of the survey overall and for each individual question. Thus we have a complete and comprehensive view of the subjective male response on these issues. This is the first time such a select group of men has been interviewed and questioned by a man to gain such an in-depth look at the male viewpoint. If you, the reader, male or female, gain a portion of the knowledge and self-understanding that I did asking these questions and answering them for myself, then this book is a resounding success. For me and my one hundred coauthors, it has been a major awakening process. We each now know so many more of our own answers and can go on to ask even better questions.

MEN ON WOMEN

1

THIS COULD BE
THE START OF
SOMETHING

"I'd been working in the office next to Alice for almost a year. I wasn't particularly attracted to her. In fact, to be honest, with her hair in a bun and her plain clothes and her glasses, she wasn't the type I'd come on to in a million years. I would stop by her office once in a while and kid around with her and the other women there, one of whom I found very sexy and took out once, but she was also very dull, so I never dated her again.

"On Valentine's Day, I sent each of the women at work a slightly risqué card as a friendly greeting. The next day, Alice came into my office and held the card in her hand and said, 'You really shouldn't send cards like this if you don't mean it.'

"She had a little smirk on her face, and, feeling my male image challenged, I responded, 'What makes you think I don't mean it?'"

"To this day, I don't know why I responded. Until that moment, I had never had any desire to spend time with Alice outside the office, though I liked her as a person and admired her competence and intelligence. Maybe it was the smirk that did it, but I do remember feeling anxious when she answered, 'In that case, why don't you stop over at my place after work? I baked a delicious chocolate cake.' Since my shift ended at 11 P.M., after work meant quite late at night to go to a woman's apartment.

"When I arrived, very nervous, because I didn't want to hurt Alice's feelings and I really didn't want to get involved with her, she opened the door and I was stunned. She had on a soft, feminine hostess gown, and her hair was falling over her shoulders, and she wasn't wearing her glasses, and the gown was molding what I could see was a very ripe and lovely body.

"After that, it gets sort of blurry. I don't remember the chocolate cake at all, but I do remember we kissed a lot and she gave me a wonderful backrub. The next night she came over to my place. It was a Friday night. She ended up staying the weekend, and we spent a very happy five years together. We only split up because she didn't want to leave the town she grew up in, and I had an opportunity to go to a much more rewarding job across the country. We still keep in touch, and I still send her a Valentine's greeting every year, even though we broke up thirteen years ago.

"She was the most loving, sensual, satisfying sexual partner I ever had. Since then, most of the women I've been with have been more physically appealing at first sight, and I've been proud to show them off. But every once in a while, I'll come across a rather plain woman and wonder."

For centuries, men and women have been trying to describe that indefinable something, that sudden knowing that here is a person you want to be with, whether for an hour or two or a lifetime. What is the spark that triggers desire? Quite often it is encountering someone who meets our preconceived notions of what will make us happy. We've all constructed certain prerequisites in our minds as to the kind of person who will fulfill our needs, dreams, and desires. These preconceived notions are usually given to us by outside sources, sources that don't always have our individual best interests at heart. Our parents, books, movies, television, magazine ads—all conspire to tell us what the perfect mate will look and act like.

And sometimes our early memories contribute to the preconceptions. Well into my thirties, I realized that there was a certain similarity in the physical appearance of the women I chose as relationship partners. This was brought home to me when I was visiting some old friends I hadn't seen in a dozen years and started showing them pictures of the important women in my life. One friend said, "They all look alike." And my other friends quickly agreed. I had never really noticed! On further contemplation, I realized that they all resembled Debbie, the most attractive and popular girl in my junior high school class. Debbie was apparently unattainable for the skinny kid with glasses who worshipped her from near, but that didn't stop me from dreaming of finding a girl just like her to love. Actually, I found several, but they didn't necessarily bring me what I wanted. In regard to this, I like Thomas Huxley's comment:

Sit down before fact as a child,
Be prepared to give up every preconceived notion,
Follow humbly wherever nature leads,
Or you will learn nothing.

I had a preconceived notion that the sensitive men I was interviewing for this book would have gotten rid of a lot of *their* preconceived notions about *who* they want as opposed to *what* they want. Some statistical surveys of the general male population have shown that the average man really has some rigid limitations when it comes to what he wants a woman to look like and act like. The men who are sharing their thoughts and feelings on these pages are not as rigidly bound. But they have certainly not given up *all* of their preconceived notions. However, they do seem to have given up enough of them to get exactly what they want for themselves. The point is this: If you are able to find your preconceived ideal of the perfect mate, then it would be stupid to let go of that ideal. But if you have spent a lot of time looking and haven't found that ideal, and have felt wonderful being with someone who hasn't nearly met that ideal, and you're *still* looking, then your preconceived notions are getting in your way.

First Impressions

A lot of studies have shown that the first few minutes of any two people interacting often determines how the entire course of their relationship will go. And yet, ironically, these first few minutes are usually filled with so many fantasies, doubts, expectations, anxieties, that we rarely see them clearly enough to get an accurate impression of what is going on. A while back, I had a very insightful conversation with noted therapist Ilana Rubenfeld on this subject. She said:

"A lot of people, as they meet each other, really see something that they'd like to see that really isn't there. What happens in the beginning is that people pretend. One part of them really knows that what they want is not there, but they pretend that somehow it's possible. The frustrations start with the other person feeling like they're not being seen, which is true, because one partner is trying to fit the other partner into a picture of what they'd like them to be, and not who they really are. A lot of the work between people has to be looking at each other the way you really are, and wanting to know if you want to be with each other as you really

are. 'Do you care for me as I really am, and not as you wish and would like me to be.' "

The way we learn anything is by paying attention to what is really happening, and if we are not happy with the results, changing what we do to *get* those results. You can't improve at tennis, for instance, if you don't think about whether or not the ball went over the net and whether you want to keep hitting it the same way or try something different. In relating to a new person—a potential romantic partner—a lot of valuable information is lost if those first few minutes are fuzzy.

This chapter focuses on what men want when they first meet a woman, when they are just beginning to know her, when they are dating, in the preliminary stages of relating. Since these are men who seem willing to make a commitment—in fact seventy-six of them are either married, living with a woman, or in what they consider to be a primary love relationship—their responses in this section tend to be clear, concise, and consistent. They *really* know what they want at the beginning, because what they want has worked for them. They've actually gotten it most of the time. Has this made them arrogant? Not according to my first question:

1. **Do you see yourself as very knowledgeable about women? Would you say you:**
   ____know all I need to know.
   ____know some, but would like to know more.
   ____know hardly anything.
   ____am thoroughly confused on this issue.

An overwhelming majority of the men responding said they know some, but would like to know more. One thirty-eight-year-old architect who has been living with a woman for the past three years said:

5

"Every woman I meet, whether romantically, in friendship, or through business, is a real education for me. I thought I knew all there was to know about women and how to get what I wanted from them when I was twenty, but a lot of pain from some relationships that ended badly got me to thinking that I didn't know anything about women. I think I was thirty when I dramatically changed my attitude and started to see each woman I met as someone who could teach me about women and about myself. It hasn't exactly been a 'free' education, but it's been worth it. And there's so much more to learn!"

2. What about a woman makes you want to spend time with her when you first meet her?

This question really goes to the heart of the matter. Is it a feeling a man gets, some kind of electrical energy, a sensory image? The responses indicate it's a combination of all of these, and it can be very exciting. Herbert, a forty-two-year-old novelist, said:

"The lady I'm currently seeing came up to me after a lecture and said she had read my first novel and wanted to give me a hug. I can still vividly remember—no, it's not even remembering, it's actually a physical sensation I can recall anytime I think of that hug. It wasn't erotic, and yet it conveyed her sexuality in a subtle but powerful way. We both knew immediately that we would soon get together and make wonderful love. Past initial encounters haven't always been so flamboyant, but there always was that special unspoken connection. It goes far beyond sexual attraction, but it's definitely physical. And if it is physical, if she touches my hand, or gives me a hug, which sometimes happens when close mutual friends introduce me to a new woman, then so much the better."

Appearance and comfort level seemed to be important factors for a lot of the men interviewed:

"Friendliness, eye contact, touching, good looks."
"Undescribable spark."

"How she appears and how comfortable I am with her."
"Attractive face. Smile. Bright eyes."
"Beauty and sensuality."
"I want a woman I feel so relaxed with we don't have to go through all the negotiation about whether we're going to have this kind of physical relationship or that kind of relationship, but we just sort of curl up together."

3. What encourages you to ask a woman out?

Though at first glance this question seems quite similar to the last one, there is actually a big difference.

The way the human mind works involves a very simple process that starts with sensory input. I see an attractive woman. This builds up excitement. I want to be with her. This takes us up to the point of the last question, wanting to spend time with someone I just met. All sorts of things can prevent my spending time with her. I may be shy, she may be unavailable, the timing may be inappropriate. If my desire does not lead to action, if I don't make a move to get to know her better, I will become frustrated and eventually build hostility toward myself or others. The cycle needs to be completed for healthy emotional response. Sensory input followed by excitement/energy buildup, followed by desire, followed by action. Not asking someone out whom you are attracted to may be hazardous to your emotional health!

I used the word *encourages* because my own experience is that I most likely will ask a woman out if something in her manner encourages me to do so, some verbal or nonverbal message says she is interested in being with me. A number of the men responding agreed.

"Encouragement from her—a smile, for example."
"My desire to, and their availability."
"A sense that she is interested and excited by my ideas and activities."
"My intuition."

"She shows interest in me."

"If she seems to be sensitive to my shyness and lets me know she likes me."

"Subliminal mutual agreement."

"If I think a friendship can develop—sexual or not makes little difference at this point, although sexual would be nice."

The more sensitive and in touch with his own feelings a man is, the more he relates to women based on how they make him feel rather than according to their meeting some predetermined physical ideal. A top television writer noted for her success in "verbal pitching"—going into a producer's office and selling him on a story—assured me that the quality of her ideas was only one factor in her success. "Everyone is insecure, especially in television, where a wrong decision can end a career," she says. "I see my job as making the producer feel comfortable—calming him down, letting him know that I'm sure this project is going to work and he isn't going to have to worry about it. If I can create a relaxing atmosphere in that meeting and convince him that my major concern is to make him a winner, then I've sold another TV movie." And at $50,000 per script, it's certainly worth the effort. I think it's also worth the effort at the beginning of any new man-woman encounter, for both persons to create a comfortable and relaxing environment. Men *want* to feel safe and comfortable. The safer they feel, the more willing they are to be open and vulnerable.

My friend Emily Coleman, author of *Making Friends with the Opposite Sex* and *Brief Encounters*, said something in one of her workshops about ten years ago that had a profound effect on me and the way I relate to women. She said that if you are feeling nervous or uncomfortable approaching a member of the opposite sex, you should tell that person you are feeling nervous or uncomfortable. This will break through a lot of barriers and make you more human. The truth is that we are all a little anxious when approaching someone who really attracts us, and if we are going to relate honestly, then *that* is information we should be willing to communicate. Chances are the other person is also feeling a little anxious, and this anxiety-in-common can create a strong initial bond.

4. Are any physical characteristics essential in a woman you'll choose to get involved with?

An overweight woman friend told me she thought a truly loving and tender man would be able to overlook her extra pounds; she didn't have much incentive to lose weight because she wasn't interested in men who picked women because of their physical beauty. Well, she may have "a long weight."

"She must be attractive, have a good figure, not fat."

"Not fat!"

"I guess a pretty face is the bottom line. A good body is a big plus, but I can be flexible and not demand a Playboy bunny if she's got a beautiful face."

"Good looks. Trim figure."

"Thin is nice. Reasonably attractive. Nice ass is a plus."

"Good legs, a sexy voice."

"She can't be fat."

"She must be attractive to me, preferably not overweight."

"She certainly doesn't have to have a perfect figure—and I have been very happy with women who might be very flat-chested or slightly chubby—but the better she looks when I first meet her, the more likely I am to get involved. And I also think a very soft and feminine voice is important, especially when she's on the phone."

The consensus certainly seems to weigh heavily—if you'll pardon the expression—against extra pounds. We are all products of conditioning in terms of what we find physically attractive. At the turn of the century, the woman considered the epitome of feminine pulchritude was actress Lillian Russell. She weighed two hundred pounds!

The best thing about this "essential" desire for a trim figure is that any woman can achieve it. Men are moving away from demanding that women look like movie stars. While earlier surveys tended to show men as very specific in their physical requirements—demanding big breasts, beautiful legs, long blond hair—the men who contributed to this book are much more flexible. I happen to know a number of the women these men are involved with or have been involved with. By movie star standards, feature by feature, some might even be considered homely, but they *seem* attractive because they *feel* attractive to themselves. And choosing to be with a sensitive man is certainly one way for a woman to enhance her self-esteem. The elimination of rigid standards of physical beauty is a very healthy development in human relations.

Women might well ask, if we men are so flexible, why are we so concerned with weight? One man, a thirty-nine-year-old ceramics artist now living with a dancer who has a plain but lively face and a very trim figure, says:

"As an artist, I have a certain aesthetic sense, and I want to feel good when I look at a woman I'm with. If she's not feeling good about herself, to the extent that she's put on a lot of extra pounds, then that affects my visual appreciation. I used to be thirty pounds overweight, and it definitely was a neurotic symptom for me. Now that I've got my body in shape, I don't really want to deal with a woman who hasn't gotten to that point yet."

Chatting on this subject with several of the men who indicated thin was in for them, I got the impression that it isn't so much a physical repulsion they feel when confronted by an overweight woman as a feeling that her extra weight is a "symptom" of some emotional difficulty. As one man put it, *"Why bother when so many women are slender out there?"*

To be fair, I must add that several of the married inter-viewees said that their wives were now overweight, though not really fat, and that this did not in any way diminish their love for their wives. A few extra pounds won't necessarily hurt a good relationship, but at the beginning, men want to start fresh with a trim body.

And remember, this question asked about "essential" physical characteristics, not for a listing of everything men found attractive. Considering this, I think it's interesting that the woman's voice was mentioned several times. One of my purposes in conducting this survey was to see if I could find some qualities attractive to men that most women weren't aware of and most men hadn't thought about much on a conscious level. I went back to some of the men who hadn't mentioned voice as important, and they all agreed that, while they hadn't thought about it very much, they were deeply attracted to women who had especially pleasing voices.

One of the keys to success in any human endeavor is to discover something that is valuable but that most people haven't yet begun to value. This is true in investing, start-ing a new business, negotiating a contract, finding a won-derful vacation spot, and being successful in relationships. While most women certainly know that being overweight is not very attractive to men today, very few seem to realize how attractive a woman's voice can be to a man. One man, a thirty-five-year-old single college professor named Jack, said that one of the women who had the most impact on him over the years was a divorced mother of two small girls who had a nice figure, a pleasant face, and the most unique and sexy voice he had ever heard.

"It had a sort of little catch in it, and a velvety sound, and it always reminded me of her lying in bed in filmy lingerie. For some strange reason, other women didn't seem to like her voice, and I've had several women friends describe her as the woman

with the strange or crazy voice. But the men swarmed around her, and she is one of the most popular women in a very competitive circle. That voice is the one thing that really makes her stand out."

Perhaps I'm dwelling on this characteristic too much, but my reasons are quite personal. I spent twelve years as a radio broadcaster. In the years since I left broadcasting, I've earned my living by communicating with other people, quite often through delivering lectures and seminars. And through the years, a good number of women have complimented me on my voice—some have even called it irresistible and told me it was the single most important factor in their initial attraction to me. With all of *this* feedback, however, I still hardly ever think about my voice or the impact it has. That is why I didn't create a question for this survey specifically asking men what they wanted in a woman's voice. So if I, who earn my living using my voice and have gotten fantastic compliments on it through most of my life, still pretty much ignore it, then there's a chance most other men and women don't think about *their* voices very often either.

The human voice may indeed be our most undervalued asset in relating to others.

In a workshop once, I asked everyone to introduce themselves by name. I taped these introductions and then played them back one at a time. I asked the other participants what image came through just from the way each person said his or her own name? Did they hear this person as confident, warm, friendly, nervous? Were they impressed by the voice? It amazed everyone how much impact the voice has. They had never even thought about this part of themselves before.

The exciting part about all this is that the voice is one of the easiest things to improve. Our vocal apparatus is, after all, a very mechanical instrument. The way our voices sound "naturally" has a lot to do with the way our parents spoke, the way we breathe, the geographical area we grew up in, and specific habits of intonation, pacing, volume control, etc. Just taping our voice over and over again will improve its quality, as we begin to correct what we don't like. For some, vocal exercises or a voice enhancement training program can do wonders. Most people's voices do not reflect how they really feel about themselves, and so do not give another person an honest impression of what they have to offer.

5. Do you find yourself more attracted to women with long hair or short hair?

Eighty percent of the men interviewed had a very strong preference for long hair. The rest said they didn't have a preference, with the exception of two men who said they *preferred* short hair. I find this interesting, in that some of the men who feel so strongly about long hair are deeply in love with women who now have short hair. This might indicate that long hair is more of a fantasy desire than an actual prerequisite, but there seems to be no doubt that a woman with attractive long hair starts out with a plus where most men are concerned.

One man, a stockbroker now living with a very attractive short-haired woman, said, *"Immediately, the idea of long hair leaps into my mind, but in reality it depends on the woman's face. Some faces are better framed with short hair than long hair. Janet used to have long hair. I've seen pictures of her then; and she's much more beautiful now in every way."*

One of the things I did as a treat for myself was to compile a photo album of the women who have been most special to me over the past twenty years. In looking through that album, I find that most of the women have had long hair, a few have had medium-length hair, and two have had fairly short hair. Both of the short-haired women were wonderful exceptions I still find very beautiful—and perfect with their hair short.

In the best of all possible worlds, we men should be able to love a fat woman with short hair, and I have no doubt that there are some delightful fat, short-haired women who could fulfill my fondest dreams. But we men are products of our cultural conditioning. We certainly are not perfect. (One of my favorite personal affirmations is: Being human is better than being perfect.) I am willing to acknowledge that, if I really had it all together, physical appearance would be meaningless. But I *don't* and it *isn't.* And while I certainly don't want a woman to want me *just* because of *my* physical appearance, I do enjoy having a woman find me attractive.

6. **Do you most often prefer a woman in a dress rather than in attractive slacks or jeans?**

Slightly more than half the men strongly preferred a woman in a dress. About 30 percent had no preference. Eighteen percent said they preferred attractive slacks or jeans. Obviously, this is not a question that lends itself to very interesting responses or comments. I only included it because I wanted to see whether the pervasive advertising showing sexy women in jeans has weaned men away from the idealized image of a woman in a silky, soft, feminine dress. Most men still prefer dresses, at least most of the men I surveyed. No real surprises here.

7. **Is there anything women do or wear to make themselves more attractive that does absolutely nothing for you?**

Research studies have shown that women dress for men, for other women, or for themselves. While the researchers can't seem to agree, most women say they would certainly change something they were doing if they found it turned men off.

When I wrote this question, I was specifically thinking of a very attractive woman friend of mine who wears much too much makeup and dresses in a sexy but not very stylish way. Whenever I've commented on her heavy makeup, she's responded that her complexion isn't very good and she needs heavy makeup. But her complexion isn't really that bad; the makeup is. She doesn't attract the men she wants and still refuses to change what she is doing.

That's not unusual. Many people want to change their results without changing what they're doing to *get* those results. And some people want to change their results without even *being aware* of what they're doing. Part of the value in this survey and in specific questions such as this one is to let women see what their results are, at least in terms of the preferences of a select group of men.

If you're a woman who is doing something a lot of men say they don't like, you can use this information to give yourself more options. If most men say they don't like the way you dress, but you have found one special man who *does*, obviously there's no reason to change the way you dress. If, however, you are lonely and not finding the sensitive, caring man you say you want, and you are doing something or wearing something most of these sensitive men say they *don't* want, some of these answers may be valuable for you:

"Perfume to excess."

"Too much makeup."

"Too much lipstick and other makeup, high heels, false anything, support garments."

"To me there is no greater turnoff than excessive makeup. Overdone blusher or eyeshadow I find makes them look like toys rather than like women."

"Dressing up too much, especially in what could be a casual situation."

"Act like 'cute' little girls and dress accordingly."

"Too much perfume makes me think they forgot to shower."

"Too flashy clothes. Heavy perfume."

"Real heavy makeup and mascara."

"Lots of heavy jewelry that I always seem to be bumping into."

"Weird-colored lipstick and eyeshadow really distracts me."

"Stockings with designs in them look silly and take away from the beauty of their legs. In fact, when I see dark stockings or lots of designs, I assume they're trying to cover up something wrong with their legs."

"Ugly shoes. Some women dress so nicely and then wear shoes that look like they came from a scavenger hunt at the garbage dump."

8. Where do you most often meet attractive women?

I asked this question because a lot of women have told me they just don't know where to find a good man. In fact, many women have asked me whether I'd be willing to share the names and addresses of the men who completed this survey. (Sorry, I promised confidentiality.)

A few years ago, I taught a course on "Singlehood: Living It and Loving It" at Miami-Dade Community College in Florida. It seemed to me then, as it does now, that one of the simplest ways to find the kind of person you want to find is to go to places where people gather who are interested in the things you're interested in. One woman who attended one of my "Love Potential" classes complained that she had ended up with three men in a row who were heavy drinkers. "Where did you meet them?" I asked. "In bars," she answered.

Now, it may be possible to meet a nice person in a bar, but it's a little unrealistic to expect to find a non-drinking person in that kind of setting. It also seems very simple to deduce that if you are interested in a person who is willing to grow, willing to be open and honest and vulnerable, that you might most easily find this type of person in a class or workshop that is teaching exactly those skills. I love reading, and mystery stories are among my favorites. There are mystery bookstores, mystery sections in public libraries, mystery writers' conferences, and at any of these I am likely to find kindred spirits. Two organizations I belong to that are just filled with beautiful, intelligent, active, exciting women are the Association for Humanistic Psychology (attracting mostly people who are teaching growth or very interested in their own growth) and the National Speakers Association (consisting of people who give motivational, inspirational, educational talks and seminars). I have never gone and would never go to a bar to meet a woman. I don't drink and would feel rather uncomfortable and silly in that environment.

The one hundred men who are sharing themselves in this book seem to agree with me. They *have* been finding women who are attractive to them in these places:

"Places of human and/or spiritual growth."

"Club Med. Association for Humanistic Psychology. Workshops."

"Any place where a commonality of interest is shared. For me, this means school, work, meditation, sports, etc."

"As an artist and teacher, I meet wonderful women at my work."

"Friends' houses. Classes and seminars."

"Meetings on subjects I'm interested in. Lectures, talks at church."

"Church and special events."

"I love comedy and am a frustrated comedian, so I go to comedy clubs and have met some really neat female performers."

"Dinner parties given by friends."

"I belong to the Church of Religious Science, a nondogmatic organization that stresses health and wealth and happy human relationships. I find the women I meet there give me just what I want in a warm, honest way."

"I like the outdoors, so the Sierra Club is a great place for me to meet women with similar interests. I also belong to a hiking club."

"I've just started getting my body in shape and have joined a local health club. There's nothing better for breaking the ice than sharing a juice drink and complaining together about your aching muscles from exercise."

"I love movies and often meet terrific women at film festivals, or even when going alone to see a movie, which I've just started feeling O.K. about doing. There are often single women in the theaters I go to, and I'll sometimes start a conversation at the refreshment stand, commenting on the film as we leave, maybe suggesting we get a snack together. When I went to see E.T. for the third time, my first time alone, I asked an attractive woman afterwards, 'Tell me the truth, did you cry?' She said, 'Yes, did you?' I admitted I had and we ended up dating. I guess not too many men are willing to admit a tender movie moment can get their tear ducts activated."

These men want women who are interested in what they are interested in, and what better place to meet them than in places that attract people with those interests?

9. **Do you want to know exactly how strongly a woman is attracted to you right at the beginning, or do you prefer some mystery, a slow unfolding of her desire or interest?**

Mothers have been telling their daughters for generations that they should keep a veil over their strong attraction to a man, that men won't value women who are straightforward on this subject. How do men committed to truth and openness feel about this ancient issue?

"I usually know how strongly a woman is attracted to me, and I like knowing."

"I like to know from the start. A little mystery is overdone, and being basically shy, I sometimes have taken mystery for rejection."

"Either way. I just need to know enough so paranoia doesn't strike."

"I can usually tell at the beginning, but slow unfolding is nice, too."

"I like mystery."

"I'm always curious about how a woman feels about me. I'm always mystified why one woman is attracted to me and another might not be."

"I prefer some mystery."

"Mystery is fine."

In light of my comments before these responses, let's underscore the fact that men were not being asked if they approved of a woman intentionally holding back information, but rather how they would like it to occur naturally. Obviously, as we become more comfortable with someone, we are more willing to communicate feelings to them, including our feelings *about* them. In further informal discussions with some of the men, they admitted that not quite knowing exactly how a woman feels is often intriguing and keeps them interested for a while. But for those relationships that become deep commitments, they like to have it all out in the open.

One of the men, a forty-six-year-old chiropractor named Henry who has been living with the same woman for six years and plans to marry her next year, said, *"A woman I really don't have that much in common with, perhaps just a physical/sexual thing, can sometimes keep me interested by playing hard to get, by not letting me know if she really likes me or when she'll want to get together again. But when there's really the possibility of a loving, intimate relationship with a woman, someone I want to share my life with, then I want to know it all as soon as it happens, and I want to tell her all I'm feeling about her."*

Another man dates a woman who is very involved with her work and other activities. She doesn't have much time for him and is rarely willing to plan to be with him even a few days ahead of time.

"Yes, it is kind of exciting never to know when she's going to call or show up. She's definitely a woman of mystery, and we have wonderful times together. But if it's ever going to go beyond playing together, beyond a once-in-a-while thing, then she's going to have to settle down and make some decisions. She sometimes says she wants a committed relationship, but her actions certainly don't indicate that this is true. And sometimes I get angry at her flitting back and forth, actually and emotionally. But when we're together and I don't try to make her be a certain way, it's very fine and very loving. How can I know how I really feel about her or what I want from her, when I don't even know for sure whether I'll see her tonight, or next week, or two or three weeks from now?"

The message I'm getting from these men is that they're willing to enjoy mystery with the women they *play* with, but want some certainty with the women they *stay* with!

10. **Think for a moment about the initial words spoken to you by women you've dated. What kinds of initial sentences were said by women that stirred your interest and led to happy relationships?**

This question was stimulated by a psychologist I heard some years ago. He said that we can often see exactly how a relationship will turn out by paying attention to the very first words spoken by that person.

"Usually something funny! Spontaneous, but funny! I like women with a good sense of humor."

"Something indicating they share similar interests."

"I was talking about my cats at a banquet dinner, and she was sitting next to me and said, 'I have a wonderful cat, too. Would you like to see his picture?' She then took out a picture and I showed her pictures of my cats. We were totally engrossed in each

other and ended up in bed together that night, at one point laughing while wondering if our cats would really approve of what they had started.''

"As a reporter, I had recently covered a story on whether local waiters and waitresses automatically gave the check to the man when a couple was dining, and this had gotten me an invite to talk to the local NOW chapter. After my short talk, one of the women came up to me and said, 'You seem so sensitive, I bet you're a wonderful lover.' I was absolutely struck mute, but finally mumbled some sort of thanks. Later on, I went over and got her phone number. We saw each other for about a year, and it was a very giving kind of relationship, both sexually and otherwise. She was a very special woman, and not really the aggressive type that I originally thought from her opening statement. I might have wanted to marry her, but she was still in love with her ex-husband and ended up remarrying him.''

" 'You do such interesting things'. . . . 'I'd really like to spend more time with you' . . . etc., etc.''

"I really get off on a woman who can just come up to me and with a big smile say, 'Hi!' This has worked out well several times.''

"Generally positive statements, talking about likes rather than dislikes. And initial honesty works well with me.''

"It was at a workshop on interpersonal communication. We were supposed to walk up to a stranger and share our fantasy about them. This very attractive blond woman came up to me and said, 'My fantasy is that I could fulfill all your needs.' I didn't end up in a relationship with her, but we had a fantastic weekend together. She lives in another part of the country, but we remain good friends, and when traveling, I'll sometimes visit her and her husband, though we've never shared with him that opening comment, which happened several years before they met.''

A number of the men said they couldn't remember any particular opening remarks. This is not extraordinary, since we don't normally pay very much attention in our initial encounters with someone new. But doing so can be valuable for increased self-awareness. Also, we can sometimes get off to a more interesting beginning if we initiate contact in an unusual or provocative way.

Some years ago, I heard Helen Hayes tell about how she met her husband. He walked up to her at a party, grabbed her hand, put a bunch of nuts into it, and said, "I wish they were emeralds." That's an opening remark no woman could ever forget! And they lived happily ever after.

I once attended a communications workshop where the focus was on the questions we ask each other. The person leading the workshop, a psychiatrist, suggested that we pair up with a partner and ask this stranger the most provocative question we could possibly think of, something we would never ask anyone out in the real world, certainly not a stranger. My partner was a very dignified gray-haired lady of about sixty-five. She asked me, "During oral sex, would you rather be active or passive?" I completely forgot the question I was going to ask her and fumbled around for a few minutes trying to answer her question, without once being able to look her in the eye! I certainly wasn't put at ease by her question, but I never forgot it, and this happened about nine years ago.

In my "Love Lab" workshops, I've often had people come up with new greetings, new ways of introducing themselves to strangers. We humans have so much creative capacity that there's no excuse for the mundane way in which we usually initiate contact.

11. What kinds of opening remarks were said by women that just didn't work out for you?

"Mainly, it was the ones who couldn't say anything."
"Something critical."

"Too ballsy, cynical, unfeminine."

" 'You remind me of my ex-husband.' "

" 'You know, if you'd just cut your hair, you'd . . .' "

"Anything boring, like, 'What do you do?' Or women who are too sexually aggressive and say things like, 'I'd like to get you in bed.' "

"One woman, after just meeting me, said, 'I'm not interested in going out with you because we really don't have anything in common.' I didn't believe her and convinced her that we should go out. We dated for about two months. I should have listened to her, we didn't have anything in common, and it was a big waste of time!"

I can identify with this last man. I think we often ignore strong indications from a member of the opposite sex that it's just not going to work out. Several years ago, I met an extremely attractive and lively woman, and almost the first words out of her mouth were, "I'm not really into relationships." I didn't really hear her. In fact, it wasn't until we broke up a very passionate but ill-fated romance nine months later that I remembered those first words.

12. **Looking back at initial contacts with women that turned out badly, do these initial experience have anything in common?**

"Yes, most of the women were too harsh."

"A strong feeling that the woman was very needy and desperately looking for someone."

"Generally, we'd get into the right/wrong game."

"Just an intuitive feeling that this wouldn't work out."

"If I've just broken up with someone and feel hurt and lonely, it seems to get in the way of being able to get close to someone. At least two relationships I started while in this situation turned out

badly for me and for the women . . . in that neither of us got what we wanted from the other."

13. Is there anything similar that happened at the beginnings of relationships that turned out well for you?

"A sense of 'preordained familiarity.'"

"Intimate conversation."

"Sharing of common interest and attraction for each other."

"We tended to do more crazy things: off to breakfast two hundred miles away, running naked in the rain at night, etc."

"Lots of honesty."

"Where the heart melts and intuitively *I feel it's going to work."*

"That sense of knowing this person as if you had grown up together, which may come from similar backgrounds or similar experiences. It feels very good, and I tend to get more deeply involved much more quickly when this happens."

There are some interesting answers from the past four questions, but I'm most surprised that we don't remember more of what happens at such a crucial time, for it would certainly help in the learning process. Of all the deeply probing questions asked of these one hundred men, these four were the ones most often left blank. So this is an area of real growth potential. Perhaps it would be useful to keep a journal of the beginnings of relationships or potential relationships, checking out what kinds of words and actions bring us what we want.

14. What would you most like a woman to suggest you do on a first date?

The men interviewed for this book seemed to like the idea of a woman suggesting what they do together on a first date. These men proved willing to let go of the old role of the man as the decision-maker in such situations.

*   *   *

"Find out about each other."

"Go out to eat and then go back to her place."

"Go for a walk in the mountains; find a nice flat rock in a stream; take our clothes off to soak up the sun; make love."

"Talk and get to know each other, then have sex."

"Take a walk."

"Go to a quiet place for dinner so that we can talk and get to know one another."

"Have a picnic on the beach, or on the floor of one of our places if it's cold or rainy out."

"The best first date I ever had was when a woman I just met suggested we go away to a cottage she had by the ocean for the weekend. I was a little taken aback at the idea of spending a weekend with someone brand-new, but the adventure of it excited me, and we managed to have a good time."

"Just spend some time together talking and getting to know each other better."

I think it's interesting that none of these men picked the all-American date: dinner and a movie. The primary concern seemed to be for some time together for mutual interaction and communication. One of the men, Harold, a thirty-three-year-old divorced industrial consultant, said:

"I'm a little hesitant about suggesting that we spend time either at my apartment or at her place, but that's what I'd like to do. Not for sex—not on a first date anyway—but just to relax and learn something about the other person. After all, what is a date all about? It's to decide whether you like the person enough to spend even more time with them. I hate it when a woman expects me to wine her and dine her and show her a good time, and then thinks she's rewarding me with a passionate goodnight kiss, or maybe even sex. It makes me feel like a paid escort, except I'm doing the paying! That's why I don't really go on formal dates anymore, but instead just suggest that we get together, maybe at the park, or some other place where we both feel safe and can get

a chance to talk. But I'd still rather she make the suggestion, make it easy on me."

15. What turns you on more for a first date, a romantic restaurant, or her cooking for you?

"Probably her cooking, since it tells me a lot about her right away."

"A restaurant. I feel a bit uncomfortable if she wants to cook for me on a first date, as if she's getting too serious or looking for a husband."

"A romantic restaurant. No contest!"

"Either one, depending on her cooking talents and on how good the restaurant is. Wherever we can get a great meal and some time together."

"A restaurant. I think if she cooked for me, I'd feel obligated to take her out to dinner another time, and I might not want to see her again."

"A romantic restaurant. I want her attention on me and not on the food and the dishes."

The overwhelming choice was a romantic restaurant, for various reasons. Some of the men said *they* enjoyed cooking for the woman on the first date. Most seemed to feel that one person cooking for another is almost too intimate an activity on a first date.

16. How can a woman touch you when you are first together that feels good and nonthreatening?

You can learn more about someone by holding his or her hand for a few minutes than by hours upon hours of conversation. In our Western culture, we are not nearly so adept at nonverbal communication as many older and wiser cultures. One of the reasons that so many people attend growth workshops and enjoy meeting people there is the permission given to touch someone, to hug a stranger, to make the kind of contact men and women often don't feel comfortable making until they "get to know each other better." Without touch, a major source of information about the other person is lost. Not everyone seems comfortable with nonsexual touching, but those who do inevitably find it easier to attract other touching, loving people into their lives.

"Massage my scalp. Hold my arm, my hand. Use touch as a natural gesture."

"Anyway she wants. Handholding, walking arm in arm."

"Holding my hand, snuggling, squeezing my thigh."

"With her eyes, her hands, and her mouth!"

"I touch her shoulder in a friendly way with my hands, and she reciprocates."

"Massage my shoulders, neck, and head."

"A hand hug [holding hands] *or placing her hand on my shoulder or arm."*

"Any soft caress."

"I can't imagine that any kind of touch from a woman I find attractive would be threatening."

"I'm not sure I can put it into words, but I love it when a woman cuddles next to me, maybe watching an old movie on TV, maybe just talking. I find that kind of warmth from a woman so appealing that I'm willing to give her anything she wants."

This area of nonsexual touching is a vital and somewhat complex one, which we'll discuss at greater length in Chapter 4. It's as if we're operating between two extremes: deprivation and being smothered. Men, like women, thoroughly enjoy a gentle and soft touch as a means of communication and affectionate sharing. But they do not like feeling "grabbed," or being touched when there is an ulterior motive behind it, such as a demand for sexual performance or for more commitment. These men seem to want some caution in their initial touching, on both sides.

17. Do you like a woman to talk openly about sex on your first date?

Women today feel much freer with their own sexuality and are much more open in expressing their likes, dislikes, doubts, and peak experiences than are men. This gives them a decided advantage when they're with a new man, since there's a good chance he won't feel as comfortable discussing sexual matters this soon. But it's an advantage that can backfire. While useful in giving women the option of moving verbal interaction to a more intimate level, it can turn some men off. It may infringe on their safety zone or confront their image of what a feminine woman should be. However, the men interviewed in this survey are more comfortable with their own sexuality than the general population, so how do they react?

"Depends on what the situation is. It would help me to learn whether she is sexually O.K. or has any hangups and is one of the 'walking wounded.'"

"Yes, but not to do it. It tells me she's an open person."

"Sometimes."

"Yes. It gets away from the game playing and it helps me do the same."

"As long as she does it in a loving way. I recently spent an evening with a woman who was telling me about her last lover and how he liked to rip her clothes off and make passionate love to her for five or six hours, and how she missed his body. Well, maybe I'm naive, but I wasn't really sure if this meant she wanted me to substitute for him or was just talking because she missed him. I wouldn't have wanted to start anything sexual with her having those kind of expectations. Even though I found her very attractive, I never dated her again. On the one hand, it made me feel uncomfortable; on the other hand, it told me right away that she and I probably wouldn't be sexually compatible, so I guess it saved me a lot of wasted time and energy. We're not all sexually

in tune, and the sooner I find out this is so, the sooner I know whether I want to keep seeing this particular woman, maybe just as a friend."

"As long as it's in context. Sometimes a woman will just blurt something out and that makes me feel put down somehow. I was with one woman—I had met her at work and on our first date, we went to a special museum showing of It Happened One Night. *Afterwards, we talked about the movies of the thirties and forties and how they were romantic and sexy without really ever showing anything. We compared this to modern pictures and somehow got on the subject of* Body Heat, *which both of us had seen. A very erotic scene has the man breaking into a house to attack the woman and make love to her while they're standing. We both agreed it was a very passionate and exciting scene, even though it didn't really show anything sexual happening at that moment. As we were discussing it, I was really feeling close to her and certain that we would go back to my house and make love. Then she said, "I've never had sex standing up and it's something I always wanted to do." Somehow this turned me off completely. It seems dumb now to think about it, and maybe I'm more uptight sexually than I thought, but it was as if it broke the mood. We* were *talking about sexy movies, but she suddenly made it very personal and almost demanding, and I was disappointed and a bit shocked. I did date her a few weeks later when I was feeling very horny, and we did have sex, but I wouldn't call it making love, and I haven't had any desire to continue seeing her."*

It's a thin tightrope to walk between having fun talking about sex or getting closer talking about sex and feeling invaded, encroached upon, or demanded upon to perform. Generalized surveys of the entire male population indicate that some men are turned on by blatant sexual talk, but sensitive and vulnerable men are not, at least not at the beginning. In further discussions with several of the participants, they told me that they do enjoy blunt talk about sex once in a while from someone they are in a relationship with, as a sort of change of pace. These men sometimes like their women to "talk dirty," but not on a first date! Most do, however, like a woman to talk about sex.

18. Do you like a woman to come on strong sexually when you first meet her?

I think it's every teenage boy's fantasy to have a woman be sexually aggressive right at the beginning—a woman who can't keep her hands off him, who can't wait to get his clothes off and have wild sex with him. Does this desire continue once we men have had sexual experience, once we've been in loving relationships, once we've learned more about our own sexual desires and needs?

"It depends so much on the woman. Some women are very clumsy about their sexuality; others are very natural. I had lunch with a woman I had just met at a morning lecture on music. It was summer, and we were both wearing shorts. We were near the Parkway in Philadelphia and decided to buy some sandwiches and have a little picnic. After we ate on the grass, she leaned over to me and said, 'I'm really enjoying this,' and then surprised the hell out of me by placing her hand on my thigh and running it up under my shorts to grab my penis, saying, 'Am I being too forward?' Of course she was, but I wasn't about to tell her. All kinds of things ran through my mind at a very accelerated pace. I mean, I hadn't even decided whether this was someone I wanted to date, let alone have sex with, so I was thrown off base by her direct attack. But I really didn't feel attacked, because she did it very softly, almost sweetly, and she was very low-keyed about the whole thing, very natural. She and I spent the afternoon in my bed, so engrossed that I missed a dinner party I really had wanted to attend—I forgot all about it. It was one of the most intense first sexual experiences I have ever had. She lives in New York, but we do manage to get together every once in a while, and I enjoy

how open she is sexually, much more so than me."

"I think it would be nice. I haven't had that experience."

"Not too strong."

"Yes and no. It depends how comfortable I feel with her."

"There's nothing worse than having a woman come on strong when you just aren't interested in her sexually. I tend to run away."

"No. That's a turnoff. I like it to build up until we've developed a good communication channel, a few dates, and then if she wants to come on strong, that's O.K."

"Not really."

"No, not if you mean in a very forthright manner . . . almost in the old stereotyped macho male way."

The consensus seems to be that a few women can bring this off so that it feels comfortable for the man, but most can't. So coming on strong on the first date is more often than not a real turnoff. My personal experience mirrors these responses. Occasionally, I've encountered a woman who's so free and easy and relaxed with her sexual nature that there's an immediate igniting of the sexual spark, but I'm not certain that could be called "coming on strong." Perhaps I shouldn't even have used that term in the question.

19. **Do you ever get the feeling from a very sexually open and assertive woman that she may demand too much from you in the way of sexual performance?**

Eighty percent of the men responding said they do get this feeling, another 10 percent indicated they get it sometimes, but infrequently, and just 10 percent say they never feel this way.

"I get the feeling that she has some real problems relating and doesn't really want to get to know me as a person."

"It's nice when a woman can be free about sex, but there are certain amenities that are nice, a certain building of warmth and communication."

"If I'm not being immediately sexual with her, then she's not really seeing me and is asking for something she probably knows will make me feel uncomfortable, or trying to control me."

"Absolutely. I think of myself as a good lover, but I'm not into entering any sexual Olympics."

We explore men's fears in this area further in Chapter 3. The indications from the responses so far are that men are fragile in this area of interpersonal interaction, and that women who are sensitive to this fragility get much more of what *they* want from these loving men.

20. **Generally speaking, do you prefer to have sex with a woman you are attracted to on your first date . . . or do you prefer to build up to it . . . touching, cuddling, getting to know each other?**

"I'd like to know as much about my partner as seems necessary before having sex, regardless of how long that takes."

"Depends on the level of intimacy and my present state."

"Building it up—it's much more fulfilling and exciting in this manner."

"The buildup. I want to know a woman before I share myself with her."

"Both. Each woman is different and so are my feelings."

"I feel more comfortable exploring and discovering. I need trust."

"I'd love to have it all happen on the first date: the buildup, the touching, the getting to know one another, and the sex; but it usually doesn't happen this fast, and the sex without the buildup is not nearly as satisfying."

"Sometimes it's perfect on the first date, but generally I enjoy getting to know each other more and building the old romantic energy up over time."

21. What is your response if a woman tells you she likes you but never goes to bed with a man until she gets to know him very well? If attracted, do you keep seeing her?

"Seems reasonable, since I feel the same way."

"Definitely, because I want to get to know her before I go to bed with her!"

"That's great and I would continue seeing her."

"I love it, because she is telling me that she is sexually willing and available if and when it feels right, which is my position, too. I much prefer this to a woman letting us go along together and then telling me somewhere down the road that she is celibate or doesn't enjoy sex at all or wants me as a friend but doesn't find me sexually appealing."

"I'll keep seeing her if attracted."

"Sure."

"Yes indeed. And it's nice to know that if we really get along together, there's a wonderful reward waiting at the end of the rainbow."

In the wake of the so-called sexual revolution, with the novelty of free and available sex having worn off, men are more interested in closeness between people rather than just between genitals. A lot more questions on what men want and don't want sexually will be asked and answered in Chapter 5. In looking at the responses to the last few questions, however, and in discussing this further with several of the men, I see that an interesting phenomenon may be occurring.

Most women think most men are more interested in immediate sex than they really are. They may be coming on strong sexually in order to please the man, even though it's not naturally part of their emotional makeup to get physically intimate that fast.

But sensitive men sense this. They are turned off when a woman seems to be pushing beyond her own comfort zone. Sensitive men want any intimate relating to be a mutual experience—mutually pleasing, mutually initiated. They want the woman to open up sexually only when she is ready to do so. This is more exciting to them; it gives them more time to explore their own feelings about this woman, more time to know what they want in this relationship.

The men I interviewed are pretty secure about their masculinity, though willing to be open about their insecurities. This security means they aren't in a big hurry to have sex with a new woman if it doesn't feel right. Security breeds patience and understanding. And these men are more appreciative of the pleasures that come with touching, cuddling—physical closeness without sex or before sex has happened. In talking to the men and in watching some of them relate to the women in their lives, I sense that they get much more physical pleasure in their lives than the traditional macho male ever experienced, no matter how many sexual encounters he had. I find this fascinating, and this is why I devote a whole chapter to nonsexual touching. Chapter 4, "Keeping in Touch," looks at how men who are sensitive feel about nonsexual touching and how they want to be touched. Remember, the label "sensitive" doesn't just mean empathetic and understanding. It means that these men are also more aware of physical sensations and better at both receiving and giving them.

22. What is most likely to turn you off on a first date?

This is information that is not usually passed on to women. It would take more than honesty to tell someone you don't want to see again *why* you don't want to see her again. In fact, most men have a difficult time even telling the woman that they don't want to see her again. Quite often, as a matter of form, the man will make some insipid attempt at courtesy by saying, "I'll call you."

Nothing infuriates or frustrates women more than having a man say he'll call but then not calling. While most men realize it's not very kind to build up false hope, they rationalize their cowardice by saying they don't want to hurt a woman's feelings. It took me years before I was able to drop the automatic "I'll call you" from my closing remarks at the end of an unpromising first date. And I still rarely feel comfortable enough to tell the woman that it just isn't working out, that it's not a relationship I want to pursue.

Though some women also hedge in this manner, I find that a lot of women are more forthright in this area than men. They can tell you they don't want to see you again without feeling guilty about it. I and other men I've talked to appreciate this honesty, even if it is at first jarring or disappointing. Nobody wants to waste time fantasizing about future plans with someone who's decided there *are* no future plans together. So here, shared in a safe environment, are some things that turn men off:

"Lack of any spark between us—it becomes quickly apparent and I don't pursue relationships where it is lacking."

"If we get into sex right away and it's obvious that we shouldn't have, our bodies just don't feel right together. Maybe, if we had spent more time together and had been more relaxed, but I never *go back for seconds under these circumstances."*

"Drinks too much! Smokes too much! Talks too much!"

"A nag or bossy woman."

"Sweaty palms when I hold her hand, which feels yucky and tells me she really isn't feeling good about being with me, or she's too uptight."

"Dull person . . . boring conversation."

"Someone who's more interested in telling me about herself than in listening to what I have to say."

"A woman who seems cold or distant."

"A woman who is very quiet and expects me to do all the talking."

"Someone who gives me no indication whatsoever that she is enjoying being with me."

"A needy woman who makes me think that almost any man would do, so that she's not with me for any of my individual attractions, but just because I wear pants."

"A woman who picks an expensive restaurant to go to without finding out if I can afford it, and assumes I will pay the check. It's as if she is trying to get as much out of me as possible, just in case she doesn't like me."

These responses, and many other similar ones not included here, all fall into the category of men saying, "A woman who doesn't relate to me as a person, doesn't keep up her end of the interaction, doesn't seem to be having a good time, isn't warm and responsive, really turns me off on a first date."

23. What factors stimulate you into wanting to go beyond a first date with a woman?

"Intellectual and animal magnetism."

"A woman who can communicate, is well read, and gives me the feeling that she likes me, and I feel that she's sensitive."

"If she shows a real interest in me and getting to know me better."

"The promise of more to come, that she hasn't told me all there is to know about her, that she has a lot of love to share and is willing to share it with me if it works out between us."

"Simply feeling good about being with her. If I feel drained or worn out after a first date, forget it. But if I feel alive and go home to bed and lie awake thinking about her, then of course I'm going to want to see her again. I probably will already have asked her out again before saying goodnight."

"Sexual excitement, any other kind of excitement, and feeling at ease with each other."

"The feeling that she has a healthy mind, body, and spirit."

"Fun is a big factor. I'm not into women who are very 'heavy' on a first date, determined to discuss serious issues or deep emotional revelations."

"A sense of immediate love or passion, or simply feeling that she's a nice person."

Herbert, a forty-three-year-old novelist who's single and currently dating someone new, wraps it all up with this comment:

"Just the feeling that I haven't gotten enough of her on a first date, that there's real depth there and something worth pursuing. And a feeling that we really enjoy each other, that we can have fun sharing all sorts of activities, and that I can learn something new from her. A feeling of liking myself after being with her and while being with her . . . that she brings out the best in me."

Though verbal and articulate on these answers, many of the men said that the real feeling can't be verbalized. It's a high level of energy and a *knowing* that this is someone you want to spend more time with. It's the feeling, in other words, that this could be the start of something . . . *wonderful!*

2

LOVE AND COMMITMENT

This chapter is all about the *something* in "This could be the start of something": a deeply committed love relationship. Most of the men have indicated that such a relationship is important to them. As reported earlier, 76 percent of them are now in such a relationship, and most of the rest are awaiting one with open arms. While a majority of those in love right now have been so with their present partner for three years or less, some of those interviewed have been married for as long as twenty-five years. So the responses come both from men who are still defining their commitments and from men who have long years of experience in successfully dealing with all the issues and changes that occur over a long-term involvement.

As we go beyond meeting someone and a first-date situation, we start to want more and we start to reveal more of who we are to ourselves and to the other person. As I gathered these answers, what began to emerge for me was a very clear picture of a group of men with higher than average self-esteem. A basic tenet in the philosophy of these sensitive and secure men is that one must love oneself before one can love another human being; love is a gift you have to have within yourself before you can bestow it or share it. To illustrate this, I asked a question that I've often asked in personal growth workshops over the past ten years:

24. **If a friend asked you for a description of yourself to give to an attractive woman for a potential blind date, what would you want this friend to tell this woman about you?**

"Good-looking, six feet tall, one hundred seventy-five pounds; romantic, caring, loving, sincere."

"Very real and genuine. Accepting, supportive, and easy to be with. Likes women who are sexually aggressive."

"I am warm and sensuous."

"Tell her about my diverse skills, talents, and interests."

"Attractive, well built, sensitive, loving, and intuitive."

"A gentle, sensitive man."

"Good-looking, very warm and cuddly, brilliant, creative, lots of fun to be with, loves to read, loves cats and good movies and good food and relaxing."

"Sensitive, caring, reasonably good-looking, tall, dark, good sense of humor!"

I find it significant—and most of the hundred men responded in this way—that even when physical characteristics are mentioned, they usually take second place to emotional qualities. Men want the women they want to *know* they are gentle, warm, sensitive.

I also found it encouraging that just about all of the answers were very positive. When I've done this question for a more general population, including men less sensitive and secure and less successful in their relationships, many of those responding tended to minimize their assets. They feared the blind date would "find them out," would consider any "bragging" a collection of lies. The 101 men we are hearing from here are not afraid of being unable to deliver on their glowing descriptions of themselves. And the women they've chosen to be with must take a lot of the credit for this high level of self-esteem. The women have encouraged their partners' sensitive natures, have rewarded them for being this way, and have modeled similar behavior to make the learning process easier.

Gary, a thirty-six-year-old medical doctor who has been married for sixteen years, says: *"Gloria really deserves all the credit for the neat man women say I am today. When we first met, I was a bit of a dolt. In my neighborhood in Baltimore, the guys treated girls like property, and this was all I had to fall back on in my own limited experience with girls before meeting Gloria in college. She didn't put up with any of that crap, which I found amazing and fascinating. I thank God I wasn't attracted to one of those insipid, dependent women, because at the time that's exactly what I thought I wanted. Hardly a day goes by that Gloria doesn't tell me I'm wonderful in some way, and I hope I'm just as supportive and caring of her. At a party, one very attractive woman flattered me by saying, 'You're the most attractive man in this room, and you* would *have to be married.' I told her that I wouldn't be nearly so attractive, because certainly my looks are just average, if it weren't for the fact I am married and to this beautiful lifetime partner."*

The first women in our lives who have an opportunity to nurture the self-esteem that leads to happy relationships are, of course, our mothers. There's a lot of blame laid at their doors, but modern humanistic psychology has discovered that those people who are most successful in life are those who can forgive their parents for any mistakes or omissions in their upbringing. "I love you, Mom, you did the very best job you could at the time" seems to be the healthiest statement we can make. But there is no doubt that our mothers have acted as role models for a good many years, and this has to have an impact on the kind of women we select.

25. Is there one attribute your mother had that you would like to see in a woman you love?

"Many qualities, none in particular."

"No."

"Supportive."

"A sense of humor."

"She was very good at encouraging my father to better himself."

"Actually there was an incredible amount of patience my mother showed me, and a whole lot of love even when she didn't understand my actions."

"She loves me. Other than that, not a one."

"Support for me!"

Our mothers loved us no matter what, and this sort of unconditional love may be exactly what we're all looking for, men and women alike. The kind of person who loves us no matter what, because of who we are rather than because our behavior meets their criteria.

In looking over the responses to this and all the other questions, I'm struck by what similar voices these men speak in, by how much agreement there is. Though many of the answers are certainly different, and the men come from different backgrounds, there are few answers from any one man that any other man could strenuously disagree with. This certainly makes it easier for me to pick representative answers, since I don't have to work hard to balance the responses I've chosen to include here; they are already very balanced and more notable for their similarity than for their discord. Since the criteria I used in asking women to recommend these men was that they be sensitive, caring, willing to be open and vulnerable, and have a history of successful relationships and friendships with women, it is not terribly surprising that they agree on many things. But even I am surprised at how very clear and consistent their answers are.

26. What one feature of your mother's personality would you most like to avoid in a woman?

"Her fear of life and inability to enjoy it."

"Her motherly role. I don't want to be 'shaped up.' "

"Dominating!"

"The critical, conservative side of my mother, limited by her religious ideas and upbringing."

"Her nasty, bitchy mouth."

"Repression of feelings."

"Unconscious manipulation."

Men want the unconditional love of a mother without the critical parent. In examining dozens and dozens of responses mirroring the ones reported above, I found a fascinating correlation between the answers to the last question and responses to the following one.

27. What one thing about you would a woman find most difficult to deal with?

The thirty-eight-year-old manager who's been married happily for fourteen years and said *"repression of feelings"* was the one quality his mother had that he would like to avoid in a woman, answered *this* question by saying, *"I find it difficult to express my wants."*

A sixty-two-year-old business executive, divorced after

twenty-four years of marriage and in a primary love relationship for the past ten months, said that what he most wanted to avoid was *"domination!"* He also said that women would find his *"fear of domination"* most difficult to deal with.

Without attempting to play psychologist with these responses, it's not unreasonable to suppose that we men may sometimes have exactly those qualities we least liked in our mothers, or have spent a lot of time and energy trying to avoid a trait our mothers had that we never learned to deal with properly. One therapist I know says that you can look at the mother and grandmother of any man or woman and tell exactly how that person operates in a relationship. I don't know if I'd go that far, but there certainly is a connection between what we want and don't want and the woman we spent our formative years with.

Some other responses to this question:

"I like things precise and orderly."

"I get bored easily in a relationship, and unless the woman is a truly multifaceted, communicative person, she wouldn't hold my interest very long."

The latter answer was from a thirty-one-year-old accountant/entrepreneur who is now living with a woman. Their relationship has been going on for about a year, and he says he's had four major relationships lasting about a year each. He's never been married. I mention all this because it puts the answer in context—showing that he indeed knows what a major issue is for him in a relationship. He knows his relationship pattern truly reflects his low boredom threshold.

"My dominance and male strength offend and threaten many women, but not the strong woman I'm now living with."

"My breath in the morning, and I pick my nose. Otherwise, I'm perfect!"

28. **What is the biggest complaint you've had more than once from women? Were they right? What have you done or are doing about it?**

No righteous indignation here! Without exception, the men all agreed that the biggest complaint from women was justified. The complaints themselves ran the gamut:

"That I don't express my wants enough. I am reading and taking workshops on this subject and now try to stay aware of when I don't share and why."

"That I ejaculate too quickly. I've tried sex therapy and lots of work on my emotions. . . . Occasionally there's progress, but we seem to slip back into old patterns."

"That I didn't pay enough attention to them. I wanted out of the relationship and wasn't able to tell them. I'm now working on not staying in relationships too long if they're not successful."

"I didn't communicate well. I now communicate much better."

"The biggest complaint I had for years was that I talked about the former women in my life. One relationship partner was so upset over this that she begged me not to keep her picture in my collection of former lovers, and this was after *we broke up. Maybe some of this was my insecurity—trying to show that good-looking and bright women found me attractive. But part of it was also a feeling of gratitude toward women who had brought so much happiness into my life; I don't feel comfortable just cutting them out. Now what I do is explain to a woman I'm getting involved with that all the women who've been a part of my life are precious to me, that I like to remember them as they helped move me to greater awareness and capacity for the love I now am ready to share with this superior woman who is now in my life. And I really believe this! Also, I am dating more secure women now, so it isn't as big an issue. I'm growing up and choosing more grown-up women to be with."*

"That I spend too much time doing my artwork. Now I spend more time with my woman."

"That I was not aggressive or direct enough by nature. I'm getting more direct but have a ways to go yet."

"That I'm domineering. I've changed my women to find those who like that quality in me."

"The biggest complaint I've ever gotten was that I don't want to make love more than once a night. I'm now with a woman who is delighted to make long, slow love just once a night."

"That I liked to flirt with women at parties and such. At first, I repressed myself, but then I figured this was going against my nature. I'm not trying to seduce these women, I just like to flirt, as they do. I'm now dating a woman who gets pleasure in the fact that I am attractive to other women. She knows it's her I'm going home with, and she knows no other woman could beat her in or out of bed."

In a relationship workshop, I once suggested that the next time each participant met an attractive member of the opposite sex, that somewhere near the beginning of their conversation, they share what it was that members of the opposite sex most often complained about in them. Not only is this a most provocative ice breaker, but if you prepare people by telling them the worst, they can't help being impressed with your honesty. They may even respond by letting you know that this doesn't bother them at all. Or, if you've corrected it, you can put their mind at ease on the subject.

The men seemed to choose either of two solutions to complaints about them. One, they recognized gripes as legitimate and worked at correcting them. Two, while they saw that the women really were sincere in their complaints, they decided they'd rather give up these particular women than whatever it was the women were complaining about. These men are willing to acknowledge their faults, but they aren't so insecure that they'll change their behavior without examining whether they really want to do so. Part of knowing what we want is being able to ask ourselves, "Do I want to keep doing this? Do I want to do something to change it?"

29. Is there anything you once wanted from women you have given up on because you no longer think it's possible or likely for you to get?

I asked this question because all of us start out in the great relationship adventure as young and inexperienced people with certain fantasies and expectations. We quite often form very precise ideas of what we want from a potential mate before we ever start relating to members of the opposite sex. As children, we are programmed and conditioned by our parents, friends, television, movies, and books to expect to find someone who can fulfill all our needs and join us to live happily ever after. Part of growing up is letting go of some of this fantasy. We're not letting go of our optimism, but realizing that we can live happy and fulfilling lives of love and joy without one person coming into our lives to give us everything we ever wanted or dreamed of from a love partner.

"As a writer, I always dreamed of falling in love with a woman writer and collaborating on wonderful books, plays, whatever. I did find one woman writer, but she had her own projects and had no desire to work with me. Actually, the one or two times I tried to collaborate with another person, it didn't really work out, so I don't know why this was so important to me. I think maybe it all came from watching two friends of my parents who owned a travel agency and worked together and traveled together and seemed to be so much in love. I really think I've given up on this one. I'm now dating a nonwriter. But who knows? If I should meet a lovely novelist or magazine writer somewhere someday, maybe the fantasy would come back just as strong as ever!"

"Someone who will not need a lot of time from me but will be

truly happy with the amount of time and attention I really would like to give!"

"I gave up a close relationship with a married woman because she just wasn't very available to me very often and had no intention of ending her marriage."

"A companion of equal intelligence and involvement."

"Yes, I've given up on finding a strong independent woman who is very successful in her own right and loves to make a home for me, is a gourmet cook, marvelous masseuse, fulfills my every sexual need, and can tune up my car!"

"No, I never give up!"

About half the men responding answered a flat "no" to the last question, as well as to the following. However, as I probed more deeply—asking the question again, perhaps giving some specific example of this or sharing one of the other men's answers—some of these men said that, on second thought, they probably had given up on something in at least one instance.

30. **Is there anything you've ever thought you wanted in a woman or from a woman, and then gotten it and found out you really didn't want it?**

The things we fantasize about aren't always going to bring us what we want. I once dated a woman who had a figure like a showgirl, was intelligent and empathetic, very sexual, a wonderful cook, and enjoyed doing things for me. I went away to a conference one weekend and she went into my apartment and totally cleaned it, scrubbing the floors, the oven, everything. It was the all-American fantasy come true, and it was terrible because she had a real emotional problem about receiving love. She could give wonderfully well but could not accept love for herself. It took all the joy out of the relationship, which lasted only about six weeks.

*　*　*

"I always was very attracted to actresses and models, very beautiful women who I imagined would give me much more pleasure in bed. But they haven't. I've dated a number and find them cold, insensitive, and completely self-centered. I'm now dating a fairly attractive accountant who just makes me feel terrific."

"I always said I wanted total emotional honesty, but when I got it, it was too intense for me. I just couldn't handle her letting me know everything she felt about herself and about me all the time."

"Long, straight blond hair. I still like to look at gorgeous blondes, but have found brunettes give me much more of what I want from a woman."

"A woman who was totally materialistic. It was fun to indulge that side of me with her for a while, but it got real boring real fast."

"Insatiable sexual desire. It became a real burden."

"Great body. It's just not that important."

"I always wanted a very sexual woman, one who wants to make love at the drop of a hat, anywhere, anytime, in all sorts of ways. Well, I got that last year, and it exhausted me. Not just the physical activity, but it was very emotionally draining and took a lot of the spontaneity out of it. I mean, she always wanted to do it, and I had to wonder if she was frustrated or disappointed when we were doing anything else. I had a pain in my penis, and the first thing the doctor asked me was if I had been engaging in vigorous sexual activity above and beyond the norm for me. It was a urinary tract irritation. I almost welcomed it as a reason to cut down on our sexual activity, even though the doctor said I could still have sex, as long as it was gentle. Never again!"

"Youth. I'm now forty-six, and in recent years, I've really been attracted to women in their twenties. But in dating several such women, I find they easily bore me, are not very sensual, are not as interesting or caring companions. I'm now seeing a woman six years older than me. She has a great body, though with some lines *in her face and some loose skin around her neck that I used to find turned me off. But she is such a great lover and so much fun to be with, and so much younger in so many ways than the twenty-five-year-olds I've met and dated, that I'm really considering making a real commitment with her, for the first time since my divorce eight years ago."*

A word here about the basic emotional conflict between *what is* and *what we believe*. Most of us go through life believing certain things will make us happy. Quite often, the real experiences we have show us that some of these things won't make us happy at all. The men who shared their answers to this last question have allowed reality to come in and replace fantasy *when such an exchange led them toward more easily getting what they really wanted.* When my beliefs get in the way of my experience, I'm asking for trouble. When I believe something or someone will make me happy, then I get what I think I want and it doesn't bring happiness but I keep on asking for the same thing anyway, then my beliefs are running my life and preventing me from getting what I want. The next question is also somewhat related to this issue of fantasy versus reality.

31. **Have you ever fallen in love with "potential" . . . with what you saw the woman becoming once she got it all together? How did this turn out for you?**

This question was directly inspired by a conversation I had several years ago with brilliant therapist-teacher Ilana Rubenfeld in New York. In fact, the following comment from Ilana forever changed the way I perceived the women in my life, changed my whole approach to relationships.

"People do see each other as potential. For instance, I could meet you and see something in you, but the timing is important.

Ten years ago I might have seen how you could be today. *And then I don't become your partner, I become your teacher. I become your teacher and your mother. And I did that with my ex-husband. I took him to the ballet. I exposed him to music.* (Ilana was a noted conductor before becoming a therapist.) *And that was putting out a lot. When I started getting back, I found I didn't like what I was getting back, and we split.*

"*In falling in love with potential—and it could be real potential . . . maybe ten or fifteen years away—I'm not really taking care of myself; I'm not nourishing myself. If I meet a person on an equal level with me, and I don't fall in love with potential but fall in love with someone who can give me something* now, *it means I'm ready to* get. *But if I'm a masochist or I'm a giver and I'm not ready to get, I'll fall in love with potential. I'll keep being a teacher, a mother, a nurturer . . . and it means* I'm *not ready to get nurtured. If I fall in love with potential, I've got to wait for that potential to come out, and it may never come out.*

"*Men who lived their potential used to scare me. I used to dream of a guy who would have a lot of money and say, 'C'mon, I'll take you to Europe for a week!' It scared me a lot. I always went out with people who were struggling. We were always potentials, all of us—potential musicians, potential writers, potential therapists. And now I'm waking up to the fact that I'm not a potential anymore. I'm living whatever I say I'm living, so now I'm looking for people who are living what* they're *saying they're living. If you're going to be with women who are strong and already there, you're going to get a lot more nourishment. Because a potential is a phantom. It may come out . . . it may not.*"

Thank you, Ilana. At the time, I really needed that. And I've played back the tape of our conversation many times over the years, when I've needed to be reminded again or when I wanted to share this powerful concept with a friend I thought would enjoy learning from it. Originally I was interviewing Ilana for a "potential" book on the ends of relationships and what to do about them. Though very pertinent to the subject of that book, what my good friend was really telling me was something I needed to hear for myself, based on what she saw me doing in my relationships at the time. In the six or seven years since then, I've gone on to other book projects. That one was shelved, but it was worth the time spent on it for getting me to think about "falling in love with potential"!

"Yes, this is a favorite number I play—not real solid ground to build a lasting relationship on."

"Yes, and it turned out miserable. I have to accept someone for what she is, not what she can become, or it doesn't work."

"Yes. It led to divorce."

"Yes, my wife, but I love each unfolding moment!"

"Yes. Not well. People sometimes don't reach their potential or cannot change their ways."

"Yes, I have a history of doing that. What happens is the woman grows and learns and gets stronger, and by the time she reaches her potential, she is ready to move on to someone else, and he gets all the benefits of all the work I put in! I get damn angry about it, and have been working at changing this pattern in my life. I'm now dating a very successful attorney, and she's helping a lot just by being who she is . . . and it feels so good!"

"I met a beautiful woman about fifteen years ago who was just entering medical school. We dated, fell in love, and married. I supported her through medical school and her internship. I really was proud of her and fantasized about being married to a doctor. I guess this is the dream of a lot of women, reversed. When she was ready to hang out her shingle, she decided that what she really wanted to do was go to a third-world country and bring medicine to people who really needed it. Intellectually, I could support this, but in reality, I had no desire to suffer among the poor. She went and I stayed. We eventually separated legally, but have never gotten around to getting a divorce.

*When she reached her potential, it just didn't turn out to be
what I wanted. I still love her, but I don't think we can ever
again share a life together."*

Sensitive men are sensitive to the reality of a situation.
They can more easily distinguish between "potential" and
what is there right now. As we reach our own potential,
we are less willing to put up with people who haven't yet
reached theirs.

Of course, someone who has arrived, who is already
accomplished in his or her actual and emotional life, has
just as much potential as someone who always seems to
stop short. The men interviewed here have all realized
tremendous potential in the past five or ten years and will
continue to make dramatic leaps forward in the next five
or ten. But they are already men of accomplishment and
creative ability and relationship success.

32. **What do you have to offer a woman that you
    didn't have, or have as much of, five or ten years
    ago?**
    "I am freer in expressing my emotions and gentleness."
    *"I think I have more maturity and experience [self-confidence]
    than five years ago. I'm probably less a romantic than before, more
    focused on career, etc."*
    "I love myself more!"
    "More acceptance and support, and I'm not as possessive."
    "Sophistication."
    "Sensitivity, consciousness, responsiveness."
    "Maturity and communication."
    *"I'm a much better lover than I was five or ten years ago—
    more sensitive to a woman's sexual and sensual needs, and I get
    more pleasure out of pleasuring her. And I've learned lots of new
    ways to gently touch and excite a woman."*

Almost all say they are much better relationship partners today than they were a few years ago. This also is reflected in their results.

33. Are you getting more of what you want from women than you did five or ten years ago?

"Yes, because I'm better able to tell a woman what I want! When I couldn't ask for it, I couldn't get it."

"Yes, more and better communication, need satisfaction, sex."

"Yes, both me and the women I meet are more sexually free and aware."

"I'm involved in the most exciting relationship of my life, but ten years ago my sex life was more interesting."

"Yes, I'm better able to ask for it and expect to get it."

"Yes, because I'm asking for more."

"Yes. When I find someone special, I'm much more able to feel at greater ranges of experience. But now that I want much more and believe I deserve much more, it isn't as easy to find someone special. I'm less willing to compromise."

This last answer reminds me of something a psychologist friend of mine once said: that the more we change and grow and become aware, the harder it gets to find a satisfying relationship partner. For many people, the myth is that the better they get at it, the easier it gets. Not true. In younger, less aware, and less sensitive years, we are often willing to settle for less than we really want. Once you've been exposed to a gourmet banquet or the possibility of such a feast, it gets almost impossible to settle for a watercress sandwich.

Some men echoed the comment from the man who reported that while his relationship is the most exciting of his life, his sex life was better ten years ago. As we learn to appreciate and express more parts of ourselves, the sexual part may no longer be as important as when we were younger. We may even choose to spend time with a partner who doesn't offer us the sexual satisfaction we had with other, earlier partners. This new partner may offer us so many pluses that we're willing to trade off sexual compatibility. Sometimes this works; sometimes it leads to frustration and hostility; and sometimes, with mutual agreement, one or both partners can seek their sexual satisfaction from others, coming back into the primary relationship for most other needs. This last solution doesn't work that often, since it requires a lot more unconditional loving, trusting, and sensitivity on the part of both partners.

We'll examine sexual attitudes, experiences, and feelings much more deeply in Chapter 5.

34. What, if any, qualities do you want a woman to bring into a relationship that you either don't have or haven't fully developed?

"Spontaneity, gregariousness."

"A greater sensitivity and ability to communicate when I have trouble opening up."

"Strong, outgoing personality."

"Maybe my ability to lovingly clean a house or take care of whatever sundry needs I have. I haven't developed those well yet."

"Emotional honesty is probably what my wife teaches me most in our relationship. At times it's all a bit too much, but I appreciate it as well."

"Tenderness, feelingness, and softness."

"Insight."

"I'm not terribly comfortable out in social situations, and the woman in my life is great at this. Whenever we go anywhere, she has no trouble meeting people and making friends, and this adds to my social success."

There's been a lot of effort in recent years to remove the disparity between the sexes. Unfortunately this has often resulted in misguided attempts to remove the differences as well. What attracts us men to women is that they *are* different. Part of our appreciation of that difference is to recognize and utilize those qualities a woman can *add* to our lives.

Most of the men cited sensitivity, outgoing personality, and a feeling, intuitive nature as the main things women bring into their lives. Milt, a forty-one-year-old design engineer who's been living with a thirty-five-year-old woman for the past six years, covered all the bases with his comment:

"I couldn't begin to list everything Marge has brought into my life. I'm a very logical kind of guy, with an orderly mind and, I suppose, some intellectual leanings. Marge is an emotional bundle of surprises who is constantly stimulating me into new creative activities, though sometimes she also irritates me with this quality. It's as if our minds mesh to create one powerful creative unit. She seems to feel more than I do in almost any situation and certainly expresses her feelings better. And she's got a magnetic personality that attracts all sorts of interesting people into our lives. I know I could survive without her, but the thought of doing so isn't very appealing."

The *differences* between men and women are also great teachers. If I had one standard that I use most often to decide whether a relationship is or was successful for me, it's whether it's taught me anything, whether I've moved forward in my growth and knowledge as a result of being with this person.

35. What have you learned from women in your life?

"How to be a more caring person."

"Everything I now know about being more human and more loving!"

"They're fun to love."

"That they are human and have the same problems as me."

"Depths of erotic feeling I never suspected I had."

"How to touch."

"To be myself and watch out for trying to please too much at the cost of really getting what I want."

"How to behave in an intimate relationship."

"How to kiss, how to cuddle, how to make love—how to enjoy it all!"

"I've learned I don't begin to know what makes a woman act like a woman, and I've learned that I don't have to understand what makes a woman tick in order to love and cherish her."

From the first moment of life, when we start learning about love from our mothers, we men are constantly sitting at the feet of the women who are our great teachers in life. There's little doubt they are better at love and intimacy than we are. It's in their genes, in their conditioning from an early age, and part of the emotions they are encouraged to feel all their lives. Men are taught to hide their feelings and go out into the world and make their mark. As long as men are taught primarily to act and think and women are taught primarily to feel and sense, we each will be teaching the other what we have learned.

36. **If you could be a woman for a day, what would you most like about it . . . least like about it? Would you be interested in dating a man like you?**

No self-image problems in this group—every man stated unequivocally that he would enjoy dating a man like himself. Empathy is one of the great human capacities, and yet we can rarely empathize with someone experiencing something we have never experienced. We can, however, come closer by pretending to have the other person's experience. This is why there's a program to have judges spend a day in jail to know and feel more about what it's like for the prisoners they sentence; why several successful high school programs have been originated to have students pretend to have a baby, taking care of an actual infant for a period of several weeks. I once attended a sexual-role reversal workshop where for an entire day the men acted the way they thought they'd act as women, while the women took what they imagined the male roles to be, pursuing the men and so forth. It was a revelation for all concerned. If we men *could* be women for a day, or even longer, we would have a greater understanding of the women in our lives *and* a greater understanding of ourselves.

This may be a useful experiment for couples to try—to switch roles for twenty-four hours. It may seem silly, but it can be a potent emotional-intellectual adventure. In unfamiliar roles, each person has to pay more attention to what he or she is thinking, feeling, doing—consciously consider a lot of action choices that he or she otherwise makes automatically. Just looking at what we men would like about being a woman can teach us what qualities we might want to try on for size. Conversely, looking at what we wouldn't like can teach us to be more sensitive to the restrictions of the female role.

"(A) Having men pursue me. (B) Being thought of as inferior."

"(A) I would like most the feelings that women are capable of feeling. I would want to be in bed with a man to see what an orgasm on the female side is like. I would like to be pretty and see how it feels to be stared at by men. (B) What I would least like about it would be my period!"

"(A) Experiencing sex from the other side. It's gotta be different. (B) Undressing and sitting down every time I have to pee."

"(A) Experiencing sex from a woman's body. (B) The physical limitations."

"(A) The softness and vulnerability. (B) The dependence and discrimination."

"(A) Emotional depth. (B) Prejudice."

"(A) Being an attractive woman and walking into a room where all the men are looking at me and wondering about me. I don't think a man ever has that power, no matter how handsome he is, unless he's a celebrity like Tom Selleck. (B) Having to put up with some of the shitty men around."

I was surprised at how many men found the idea of experiencing sex as a woman so appealing. And they certainly seem aware of some of the complaints women have today. If there are two things men envy women most, it's their sexual capacity—the passion of their orgasms—and their emotional vulnerability. And it may be exactly these two areas that threaten men the most. (More about this in the next chapter.) But it does seem to be an essential part of our natures that we are quite likely to be very attracted by that which we fear. I well remember my teenage years of shyness, when girls fascinated and terrified me at the same time. I think many of the responses these men have shared, particularly in the next chapter, "Fear of Female," reinforce the idea that women, in a sense, represent for men what the flame represents for the moth: danger and desire. There's a constant dance consisting of moving toward and then pulling away from the object of one's desire.

Let's look at some things that move men away.

37. What is one habit that a woman you've been interested in had that really turned you off?

"Talking only about herself and not being interested in me!"

"The habit of inflexibility, having to have things her own way."

"Holding on to her anger until it explodes."

"Eating sardines in mustard . . . the idea of it made me sick."

"Spraying perfume on the pillows when she was feeling sexy. It was so corny, and I felt like a performing seal who had

to respond to signals whether he wanted to or not.''

"Yelling and screaming about some hurt or imagined hurt and then wanting to make love to make up when I was still feeling upset and withdrawn.''

"Always writing in her journal after we made love and never letting me see it. It really got to annoy me, as if she was preparing reports on what we did.''

"Keeping the door open when she was on the toilet, as if I somehow found her elimination processes sexy or romantic. I didn't.''

"Picking at the food on my plate at a restaurant, especially when she would say she wasn't interested in ordering something and then would end up eating most of mine!''

"Making a point of paying her own way when we were with other people but expecting me to pay when we were alone, so that all her friends thought we always went dutch, when I usually paid.''

A litany of grievances, both trivial and substantial. We all have things that annoy us about someone we love or someone we find attractive. Once they're out in the open, they lose a lot of their negative power. One woman I was with taught me a valuable exercise when she suggested that we tell each other three things that annoyed or irritated us about the other person. Of course, I don't recommend trying this unless the relationship has already achieved a certain level of trust and communication.

Habits are, by definition, things we do repeatedly and automatically without conscious thought. Just becoming aware of some of our habits can eliminate them, and one very loving function a relationship partner can perform is to point out some of our behavior patterns, some of the things we do unthinkingly that don't serve us well.

38. What bores you most in a woman?

"Immaturity, talkativeness, gossiping."

"Nothing. Boredom comes from within. If I am bored, that is my fault, not the woman's."

"Loud and boisterous behavior."

"One who consistently talks about herself or who talks about something boring constantly, no matter how much you tell her you are tired of hearing about that subject."

"Talking about superficialities."

"Poor conversation and negative attitudes."

"A woman with a limited number of interests and yet an overpowering priority that everything be done together and in the context of a 'relationship.' "

"Storytellers who continually talk."

"Talking about people I don't even know and who are not even interesting."

"One woman I dated was an actress who had been in one Broadway play and never stopped talking about it even eight years later. At first, the stories were interesting, but she told them over and over again to anyone who'd listen, and it was like the old veterans who keep on talking about the same battle. Boring!"

"Talking about her ex-husband or ex-lover so I almost get to know them better than I get to know her!"

"Telling me about the intimate details of her life and health. I don't need to know that she had a vaginal irritation two years ago, that she's been constipated all week, or that she's trying a new shampoo."

Interestingly enough, none of the men said they were bored by a woman who was quiet and didn't talk enough. I used to do quite a few workshops for singles groups, and at one of them, I told the men and women that one way to avoid being a bore was to do a spot check before saying anything. Ask yourself, "If someone were telling me this, would I find it interesting, exciting, or would it tell me anything important about him or her?" Perhaps I should have asked the men what they think *they* do that's most boring. And perhaps in another book, the women will tell us!

After these particular answers, an obvious next question is:

39. How important is it that a woman be able to carry on an intelligent, interesting conversation?

"Very important."

"I think it's more important that she's having an interesting life, and the conversation will follow."

"On a scale of one to ten, nine."

"If she can't, I refuse to be with her."

"Absolutely vital!"

"I doubt if I'd even get to a first date if she didn't."

"I have been turned off by so many beautiful women who haven't an interesting thought in their head that I sometimes think I ought to settle for some dumb but sexy woman and just talk to myself!"

This would appear to be precious information for women. So many millions of dollars are spent by women to improve their bodies, their makeup, their clothes. Just a fraction of this is spent on improving their minds and expanding their horizons. In all fairness, most of the men interviewed report no trouble at all finding bright, witty, interesting women to relate to, and I think there are many more such women out there now than in previous years. Nevertheless, I think it's important to note that sensitive and caring men do not want to be bored. If a woman has had trouble attracting such men into her life, she might check out whether she's an interesting conversationalist. One final comment on this subject:

"There's nothing worse than lying in bed with a woman after

making love and finding she has nothing even the slightest bit interesting to say. I love talking into the wee small hours with a lover."

40. **What are some things you've endured but not enjoyed because you thought a woman expected you to do so?**

"Visits to in-laws."

"Parties, her friends and family, movies, etc."

"Long, drawn-out discussions into the night, trips to friends' houses to visit with them when I really felt like being by myself, staying home when I'd like to be elsewhere."

"Waiting. Shopping."

"We're in an open marriage, and some of the guys she's chosen to go out with have really pushed my buttons."

"I went into therapy because she wanted me to, and I think it was a total waste of time, with a really incompetent therapist whom she raved about."

"Nothing now. When I was younger, maybe a few things— like going to lectures or concerts I really wasn't interested in."

Fewer than half the men questioned could even come up with something they've unwillingly endured, and some of those who once did said they didn't anymore. These men are *not* willing to put up with things that don't interest or pleasure them just because the woman in their life expects or requests or demands it. Growing is really a form of waking up, and the more we wake up, the more precious we consider our time and the less willing we are to use it in unproductive, unpleasant, or boring activities.

That brings us to the longest question in the survey.

41. **What is the ideal amount of time you want to spend with a woman who is important to you? For instance, would you enjoy working together,**

sharing twenty-four hours a day? Or, assuming she would be equally happy with the arrangement, would you prefer someone you just see evenings and weekends . . . or just weekends . . . or one weekend a month and one or two evenings? If you could choose, what would be the ideal time commitment on your part?

The time we spend with a relationship partner is very rigidly bound by certain cultural conditioning. We date someone, begin to feel close, begin to fall in love, and pretty soon we're seeing that person every waking moment, even if this is not the ideal amount of time for us to be spending together. Each of us is very individual in terms of how much companionship we need, how much time we need to be alone or working or playing with people other than our love partner. Any two people have a certain energy exchange between them, and it may be that this energy is so intense that seeing each other once a week gives the nourishment they need and want in a relationship.

But we are so conditioned automatically to spending weekends with someone we love that we may ignore what really feels best for us. I dated one woman who was beautiful, sexy, loving, intelligent, adventurous, and loved to spend a full twenty-four hours with me—walking on the beach, making love, massaging, cooking a meal together. It was as if we spent a month together in that intense twenty-four hours, and neither of us had any need or desire to see the other for a few weeks after one of our magical days.

Other women in my life, not as intense, I could enjoy seeing more often. One woman I lived with was truly enjoyable twenty-four hours a day. But I can't say I got more out of living with her day and night for three years than I have from seeing this other woman for intense twenty-four-hour periods a few times a year. The point is that we have to pay attention to learn what the ideal time frame is for any relationship. Ignoring this can often end a very loving experience before its time.

"Depends. Probably evenings and weekends."

"I think a very flexible schedule. Probably sleep together nights, but be used to a few days of time apart, with intense times together —maybe alternating a few days together with a few days apart. I'm not big on regular schedules."

"Twenty-four hours a day may be a bit much. I enjoy living together. Spending most of the weekends but not all, due to my sports and exercise activity, and two to three evenings a week. I perceive a healthy relationship as having outside interests which are individual but brought back to the relationship to enhance it."

"Full time, as long as she's in a good space emotionally."

"Mornings, evenings, weekends, and vacations."

"Evenings and weekends."

"Marla and I do just about twenty-four hours a day, and it works. Haven't met anybody else that I've felt I could enjoy that much."

"We get together one or two evenings a week, and she likes to spend Friday night with friends and Saturday with her kids, so she comes over Saturday night and stays until she goes to work Monday morning. I like that solid amount of time from Saturday night to Monday morning. It's like a small vacation, and it gives me Friday nights free to do whatever I want and Saturdays to relax and do any chores that need doing."

"I never know when I'm going to see her, as she travels and has a very busy schedule. Sometimes she'll drop by out of the blue at midnight and spend the night; sometimes she'll show up at 5 A.M. on Saturday morning to wake me up with kisses and ask me to watch the sunrise with her. At first this nonstructured, unscheduled stuff drove me crazy, because I've always been used

to setting a time and place to get together ahead of time. But I really enjoy being surprised now. She even came over one evening to take me out to dinner, and I had another woman friend over. She took both of us to dinner and then said goodnight and left us. I wish I could be as free as that. I think I'm learning a lot about how hung up I've been about scheduling all my life. It still makes me uncomfortable sometimes, especially when I want to see her and don't know when I'll see her. But the pluses outweight the minuses most of the time."

It seems that most of these men still feel most comfortable with evenings and weekends spent with a partner, which is generally true for people in our culture. But they seem more accepting of nontraditional time arrangements and more willing to experiment in this area.

42. **Do you ever spend more time with a woman than you would ideally choose, because she seems to want this? How does this feel, and what does it usually lead to?**

"Yes. It makes me feel confined and usually ends with me splitting."

"No. I make the choices as to time I desire to spend with any woman. If she gets possessive, I don't appreciate it and we usually say good-bye, or at least I say good-bye."

"Yes. I feel frustrated and resentful."

"Yes. It's like being in a straitjacket, and it's so hard to tell her I want to spend less time without hurting her feelings. Out of frustration, I end the relationship."

"Yes, and it usually leads to my not really being with her totally even when I'm with her. This happens to be a big issue in my life."

"Yes. It feels bad . . . like a duty or obligation. It leads to resentment and distance between us."

"Sometimes, and when I don't want to be there, I just tune out and daydream."

Only about half the men responded by saying this was true once in a while. A few stated it wasn't, that they never spent time they didn't want to spend, and the rest didn't answer the question, indicating it's not an issue for them. As we get more self-supportive, we tend to eliminate "giving in" to someone who wants something we don't want to give. The few men who indicated this was a big issue were all married to very strong women who sometimes wanted them around when they didn't want to be there. One man who's been married seven years told me that a big problem is the fact that his wife, a writer, has a very quiet day of work, while he, a motivational speaker, has a very busy traveling schedule. When he comes home, he wants to curl up with his wife and a book in bed; she wants to go out and visit friends or go to parties or have a night out on the town. They've compromised by his taking her out on one exciting weekend trip each month, while she gets into making him as relaxed and comfortable as possible when he comes home from the road. This kind of balancing act is necessary when two people spend their time apart in such different ways that they need different things from each other when they are together. But other couples just go along resenting each other without ever dealing with the problem and allow a lot of anger to build up.

43. Is there anything you expect a woman to give up in order to be in a relationship with you?

"Sex with others."

"Her belief that every relationship has to lead to marriage or end."

"I expect her to stop looking for other men, but she doesn't have to give up her male friends."

"Other men."

"She shouldn't have to give up anything besides other new relationships in her life (except friends)."

"Other lovers."

Almost universal agreement on this. With one or two exceptions, the men all seemed to feel that other sexual relationships were all they'd ask a woman to give up.

About 40 percent of the men said there wasn't anything they'd ask her to give up. Not wanting to assume that this meant they felt O.K. about her having other lovers, I checked this out with a sampling. About two-thirds of those I talked to said they just assumed she would not have any other lovers, so hadn't thought of this when answering. The other third said they'd feel fine if she wanted to keep other lovers, as long as they had the same privilege. Remember, this is one-third of a sampling of the 40 percent who hadn't said there was something they would expect her to give up. This would come to thirteen or fourteen men out of the 101 men participating. These responses are also indicative of the fact that these men are more accepting than the average man of such things as a woman's friends, other interests, career, etc.

They may be more accepting, but there are limits. While the men interviewed seem to be happier than most about their love relationships over the years, they all have had relationships end. In asking the following question, I wanted to underscore the fact that a relationship's ending is not synonymous with relationship failure. Just as there are different ideal amounts of time for two people to spend together *within* a relationship, each relationship has its ideal lifespan—a certain length of time when it is mutually nourishing. I like a statement made by the well known minister-teacher Reverend Terry Cole Whittaker: "I would rather spend one year in a 100 percent committed relationship than thirty years in one that's only 30 percent committed."

As in any learning, the way we improve at relationships is through building on a history of ones that didn't continue, for whatever reason—going on to new partnerships that give us more of what we want, until we find one that allows us the space and emotional nourishment to grow and learn *within* the relationship, one that accommodates itself to our changing needs, feelings, and perceptions.

44. What is the major thing that made you want to end the relationships you've ended?

"There just didn't seem to be solutions or enough energy to keep looking for them."

"Differences that have developed in our lifestyles. Lack of communication used to be a major problem."

"Women without a backbone, without a sense of purpose or mission, without their own identity."

"I've gotten out of relationships when women were being cling-ing, cloying, when I felt I was being emotionally, physically, mentally sucked on, in a draining, parasitic sort of relationship. I walked away from the relationship with my ex-wife because it was psychologically brutal and devastating. . . . When I get to a point where there's just no love feeling left, I leave."

"Judging and blaming me, or where we point the finger back and forth."

"I would get clear after a couple of years that this wasn't the person I wanted as a life partner. In one case, our sex life wasn't compatible. There's almost been a different reason in every case. In each one, though this was a pleasant person, it wasn't who I wanted for a life partner, and I felt I was wasting all this time building intimacy with a person whom I wasn't going to be with a long time anyway, so I may as well end it."

"The feeling that I wasn't really being seen as a person, just as a male presence. My last relationship lasted almost three years, and I ended it when I saw clearly that she wasn't so much in love with me as in hate with the idea of being alone. Sure enough, the idea of being alone so terrified her that she was in another rela-tionship within two weeks, and she's since married the guy."

"Too much dependency—neediness."

"Lack of interest in continuing some, and fear in others."

"Disagreements as to values. In the one before my current relationship, she wanted to live in the country, and I wanted to travel most of the time."

In building a storehouse of information to draw upon for successful relating, it can be very useful to know exactly why certain relationships ended. It's important to learn from each relationship.

Though we sometimes dwell more on the things that don't work than on those that do, it's really more important to look at past relationships in terms of what was wonderful and nurturing about them. A useful technique I've suggested to couples who've decided to go their separate ways is one I used myself at the end of a particularly joyful relationship. At the time, it wasn't a technique, just something it felt right to do. I sent Bonnie two letters in the same envelope. One, about two pages long, listed the things I was hurt and upset about in the ending. The other, five pages long, enumerated all the joys and pleasures I had experienced during our three years together, including some of the things I had never gotten around to telling her while we were together. These included the pleasure I used to get just watching her sleep—she had the most peaceful, beautiful expression on her face when sleeping. I think this sharing of the good as well as the bad helped us remain good friends through the years. Eight years after ending our relationship, we still haven't ended our love for each other.

If I had it to do over again, one question I would add to the survey would ask the men if they still remain friendly with ex-relationship partners. I already know that a good many of them are, since I either know them or they were specifically recommended as wonderful men *by* their ex-partners. This ability to keep some of the love alive even while the relationship itself is dead is a mark of sensitivity and maturity. Of course, both people have to be willing to reach out and go beyond any temporary bitterness or hurt or blame. In four major love relationships over the past twelve years, I remain dear friends with two of the women and have had almost no contact with the other two, as they just preferred going on with their lives and loves without me.

Considering that we can learn more from what goes right in relationships than from what went wrong, . . .

45. What is the main thing you want from a woman you want to spend time with?

"I want to share openly with her and she with me."

"Companionship and sex."

"Unconditional support no matter how crazy I am."

Sometimes a work schedule has a lot to do with relationship needs, as in this comment from a thirty-five-year-old single composer-producer who is dating, among others, the woman he lived with for two years:

"Intimacy is very important to me. I don't work a nine-to-five job, and most of my friends don't either. I'm very busy, and I don't have a lot of time for a lot of intimacy with a lot of people—not as much as I'd want to. It's nice to have one person in your life who's not only involved in all the physical details of your life but also knows you emotionally and mentally. And it's very nice, since we all have sexual needs, if that's also the person you go to bed with at night and you have that interchange of what's going on in your life and what's going on in her life—sharing emotional perceptions of what's going on, and kind of bouncing your lives off one another in an intelligent, stimulating way . . . which always feels better after sex anyway."

"Sex would definitely be one thing, and one reason I would choose to be with one woman as opposed to a bunch of women

would be that the sex was very unique, very individual, with very compatible sexuality. Also, a mutuality of involvement in life, of involvement in career—I couldn't be with someone who was just vegetating in a career, vegetating in her life, because I'm not. That sort of co-existing involvement, yet a separateness—more like two people walking along the same road together instead of Siamese twins."

"I would have to say sex, in that that's why I would choose to spend time with a woman rather than a male friend."

"In a love relationship, it would have to be a good cuddling, sexual connection . . . this being the main thing that would separate it from a loving friendship with a woman."

"Understanding and acceptance, that she would be interested in my thoughts, interests, and ideas and brainstorming, and feelings and activities, and that she would share deeply what was going on with her in all of those same things. That she would be stimulating to me, with a mutual growth process, so we both would be growing as people. I definitely wouldn't want someone who wasn't changing and growing and developing. I also want someone who would share domestic chores with me—cleaning up, laundry, etc. Sex is certainly right up there, but I'm sure it's been well covered by the other men. Even ahead of the sexuality, though, would be a mutual attraction toward each other—somebody I could have fun with, play with, and laugh with."

"I want to feel comfortable with her and not feel like I have to put on an act. I'd like her to be equally comfortable with me. I don't like game playing."

"She should be passionate, very sexual, involved in her own life, and an interesting companion."

"I want a woman I feel so relaxed with we don't have to go through all the negotiation about whether we're going to have this kind of physical relationship or that kind of relationship. That we feel so naturally blended together, we just sort of curl up together as a natural, organic process. And I want a woman who is capable of surprising me, because I have a very low boredom

threshold . . . I've only lived with one woman who constantly surprised me and she also drove me crazy. And someone whom I respect and who creatively stimulates me, whose work I can enjoy and get enthusiastic about and appreciate."

A number of the men, twenty-eight of them, just answered with the single word: *sex.* I appreciate their honesty. I was actually somewhat surprised by the emphasis on sex in almost all of the answers. On reflection, I don't know why I should have been. Perhaps it stems from some mythological assumption that "sensitive" men should be interested in "more important" things, such as intellect, warmth, etc. My thinking can sometimes be as limited and narrow as anyone's.

What higher purpose could any man aspire to than a healthy sexual relationship with a woman he loves? Also, since most of these men feel very comfortable having very loving nonsexual friendships with women (a number of them being recommended for this survey by these women friends), then obviously sex is the one thing a love partner can add to their lives that they aren't getting from their friends. This may also shed light on why most of these men seem so satisfied with their lives and feel loved and accepted. They *do* have women friends and therefore are not dependent on a relationship to bring them everything they want from a woman. When not in a relationship, therefore, they do not become needy or desperate, the sure way to attract an unhealthy relationship partner. Men who can relate to women as close friends have it all over men who can't and are much more successful in life and in relationships.

The men I interviewed seem very based in reality instead of fantasy, as illustrated by the fact that the following question was a complete dud in terms of getting any interesting answers:

46. **Are there some ideal women you fantasize about —movie stars, someone you once knew . . . maybe someone unavailable, like the wife of a friend?**

The interesting thing here is that, without exception, the men responded with "No!" "Not really" "No" and "No, not really." Earlier surveys of broader-based male populations indicated that those responding fantasized a lot about their ideal woman. I suspect the difference is that the men interviewed for this survey *are* successful in their real relationships and have no need to fantasize.

47. **Other than sex, what do you see as the most important thing a woman can add to your life?**

"A different point of view."

"She can assist me in understanding myself."

"Companionship and friendship."

"Companionship and sharing. Also, I find women in general prettier to look at than men."

"Someone to share life's hassles with."

"Organization. My life is a mess without a woman!"

"A sounding board for my ideas, dreams, and memories."

"Someone to listen to me, really listen."

Of course, by offering expanded answers to Question 45, many of the men already covered this topic. Most often they seem to view sharing, listening, companionship, and friendship as the important nonsexual needs of a relationship.

48. **If you could choose three things that a woman should be able to do exceptionally well, what would they be?**

"Run her own life, make money, and love me."

"Be sensitive, be supportive, be able to carry on an intelligent conversation."

"Enjoy her work, play, make love."
"Think, feel, and love."
"Sex, dance, cook."
"Sex, listen, communicate."
"Make love, think, talk."
"Cuddle, have sex, love me."

Through all of the responses, it seems clear that men want women to be bright, thinking, feeling, loving, and very feminine people. What we really want is a very visceral thing, and even these men, who express themselves so very articulately, don't reveal exactly what it feels like to have what you want. They express it better than most —we can get a very strong sense of what it is they really want—but we really only know what we want when we actually get it. And each time we get it, we add more information to our memory banks, so that we know a bit more of what we want.

At one point in my life, I thought what I wanted from a woman was total sexual compatibility and a loving, nurturing person who supported me in everything I did, who was beautiful and was someone I would be proud to be seen with. This was, therefore, what I looked for in my next relationship. But when I met my next relationship partner, she was not quite as sexual as my last partner had been. She *was* physically and emotionally powerful, and was as voracious a reader as I was. She loved getting up early in the morning for two sets of tennis and a swim and then cooking a magnificent breakfast, and then going back to bed and making love. This was a totally new pattern for me, but I loved it, and all of a sudden I had a new idea of what I wanted in a woman.

The next woman in my life told me she liked to play tennis. Since I had never really been into any sports, I felt my former partner had opened up a whole new world for me. But once this new woman and I got deeply involved, she tired of tennis and didn't want to play anymore. And she wasn't nearly as sexually compatible with me as the two earlier partners had been. However, she had the most stimulating intellect I've ever encountered in another person, and was the funniest, cuddliest, most interesting person in the world when she woke up in the morning. She also loved animals as I did, and loved browsing in bookstores. I fell deeply in love with her, despite the fact that she wasn't able to give me what I thought I wanted, based on my earlier experiences of getting what I wanted.

The point of all this is that what we want is not a precise, specific thing so much as it is a textured tapestry of experiences spread out over a lifetime, including many interpersonal interactions. That is why I've asked all these questions, instead of just "What do you want from a woman?" Each of the respondents can only answer from where he is right now. Next week, or next year, a new event or new person may broaden his perspective—provide new information on what is wanted, perhaps in addition to what he now has or has had in the past.

Maybe it all does boil down to what my friend, Ken Keyes, Jr., author of *The Handbook to Higher Consciousness*, says: "Everybody wants love." No matter what they're saying, doing, being, every single man and woman wants love in his or her life—wants to feel love, wants to be loving.

Ken Keyes, Jr., also said something in a workshop I attended that led to the following question. He said that what was important for him was to have a partner he could just *love to be with*, rather than trying to find someone to do things with, like go to the movies, eat out, whatever. Those were things he could always do with friends or even acquaintances and didn't need a relationship to have.

49. Do you usually choose a woman you can do lots of things together with . . . or a woman you enjoy just being quiet with?

"Both. One of the lots of things we like to do is be quiet together."

"A woman I can just enjoy being with, without having to do anything."

"I'm dating a woman now who is always wanting to run and do something, and I miss someone to just cuddle up with in front of the fireplace, to lie in bed with just talking about this and that on a Sunday morning. So I'm still looking for someone who just enjoys being with me and me being with her, without having to say a word, but free to say whatever we want, and certainly without having to run and occupy our time with 'doing things.' I think it has to do with her self-esteem. It's as if she can't consider herself worthwhile unless she's accomplishing something. She's a workaholic and a playaholic. Maybe she's afraid that just being herself with me just being myself will somehow cause her to fade into the woodwork."

"Just being quiet with her is what being together is all about . . . if I can't do that, then why bother?"

"I want someone I can do things with. I can be quiet by myself, but I want someone to share the activities I enjoy: running, swimming, going to concerts."

Ten percent of the men said they prefer someone they can do things with. Sixty percent said they want someone they can just enjoy being with. The rest said they either didn't have a preference or wanted both. These are not mutually exclusive items, of course, but what I was looking for here was the primary focus in choosing a partner. Those men who, judging by their descriptions of themselves, seemed to have a full life with a lot of activities and lots of friends, inevitably chose to be with a woman they could just enjoy being with. Those who led quieter lives, were in less active careers, and seemed more insecure about their self-worth wanted a woman to share lots of activities with them. They would choose this kind of woman over one whom they could just enjoy being with. A higher proportion of the men who said they were primarily interested in doing lots of things with a woman also said they had difficulty with intimacy, that they tended to pull away if a woman got too close or too "possessive."

50. **Do you enjoy being surprised by a woman, or do you feel better knowing what she is likely to do in most situations?**

I asked this question because it also has to do with our inner security. A lot of the men said that it's important they feel comfortable with a woman. But is comfort such an issue that they don't want the boat rocked with surprises? Certainly not with this group of men!

"I like surprises."

"I always enjoy a pleasant surprise."

"I don't want to be surprised about how she feels about me, but in all sorts of other things, the more surprises the merrier."

"I don't like too many surprises right at the beginning of a relationship, but after we get to know each other and feel good together, I like spontaneity and the unexpected . . . though I don't mean the kind of a surprise where she doesn't show up for an expected date, or where she decides to go out with another man instead of me. I mean surprises like her showing up with a batch of cookies she's baked, or taking me to a wonderful lake she's discovered, or planning a surprise trip for us!"

With almost no exception, these men like being surprised. And they like surprising their women. One man, a forty-year-old television script consultant who has been living with a woman for the past two years, said:

"One of my biggest disappointments is that she doesn't enjoy surprises. She wants to know where we're going for dinner and what the selections will be. She wants to know ahead of time what I'll get her for her birthday, and she doesn't even seem to enjoy it when I bring a surprise gift home spontaneously. I once bought some roses and brought them home, and she said, 'You should know by now that I like plants and not cut flowers!' It's the major issue in our relationship and the one thing that would make another woman attractive to me. Maybe it's an ego thing, but I love being able to think up wonderful surprises to deliver to someone I love, and I feel really stifled now."

51. What kind of response do you want when you do or give something nice to a woman?

"The truth? I want her eyes to light up, have her squeal for joy, throw her arms around me, and drag me off to bed to make mad, wildly abandoned love to me!"

"I like loving appreciation. Verbal is enough."

"Recognition and a thank-you."

"Appreciation, naturally."

"An honest one."

"Excitement and a happy response."

"I want her to be thrilled and feel very loving toward me."

I somewhat suspect that the first response above might be the most honest. Being less than perfect creatures, we all expect something in return when we give something to someone we care about. Do you really think you'd want to keep giving wonderful presents to or continue doing wonderful things for someone if the response you got was an indifferently mumbled "Thanks"? Part of the joy in giving is in anticipating a joyful, appreciative response.

Now, if you're in a deeply committed, loving relationship, once in a while you might give something or do something for your partner that falls short of the mark.

Certainly there is room in this kind of relationship for honestly expressing yourself when what you get doesn't excite or please you. But remember, the question isn't what kind of response the man is willing to settle for, but what he most *wants* the response to be. When I give something to someone, especially if it's a surprise, I can certainly live with the reality that once in a while it will be greeted with less than wholehearted enthusiasm. But I *prefer* that I get a much warmer reaction.

In workshops I've conducted on giving and receiving, I've often found that childhood patterns are reflected both in the way we give to others as adults and in how receptive we are when receiving from others. A successful love relationship is most likely when both partners are good givers *and* good receivers.

The Giving and Receiving of Compliments

One area of human interaction that provides an accurate indication of our ability to give and to receive is compliments. There is a direct correlation between our ability to give and receive compliments and our ability to give and receive love, money, honesty, etc. If I can receive a compliment without diluting it by feeling obligated to return one immediately or by deprecating myself ("What? This old jacket? I've had it for years!") and simultaneously insulting the taste or judgment of the person paying the compliment, I am probably the type of person who feels deserving of praise and deserving of love, willing to accept both from other people.

All of the men said they enjoy praise from women. About half said they now get enough praise from women. The other half said they'd like more, and they had very specific ideas on what they wanted to hear and were well aware of what women did like about them:

52. What would you most like a woman to compliment you about?

53. What do you most often get complimented on?
It seemed most interesting and useful to combine the answers to these two questions, to see if these men often get what they want in praise from women.

"(52) My sensitivity and ability to love. (53) My sensitivity."

"(52) That I'm really a fascinating person. (53) That I'm a great listener."

"(52) My sensitivity. (53) My lovemaking ability."

"(52) My brilliance and what a good lover I am. (53) My strong, masculine nature (except by those women who are threatened by it)."

"(52) Being a gentleman and a nice guy. (53) Being a gentleman and a nice guy, my eyes, and being cuddly."

"(52) Being wonderful to sleep with all night. (53) Some compliments on being great to sleep with, but most are on my sensitivity and vulnerability."

"(52) My work toward emotional honesty. (53) My work, period."

"(52) My talent, ability, feelingness, sensitivity, and looks. (53) All of the above."

These and most of the other responses indicate that while these men don't always get exactly what they want in a compliment, they do enjoy the ones they get. I think most men tend to take their women for granted, in that they forget to pay compliments on a regular basis. This survey shows that women often do the same. We forget the power of praise, the life-affirmation we get from hearing another person express pleasure about something we are or something we've done. One way to facilitate such an exchange in a love relationship might be to tell each other what you most enjoy being complimented on. Share what would prompt each of you to compliment the other in this desired area.

Of all the strategies for positive action I have shared in my books, workshops, and on my tapes, one of the most popular, in terms of people reporting back that it had a major impact on their lives, is one of the simplest. I started following this strategy myself about three years ago, and it's been very rewarding for me.

Whenever someone pays me a compliment that feels especially good, I ask them to put it in writing and sign it. Then I put it up on my Compliment Bulletin Board. What this does is perpetuate the good feelings emanating from the compliment, far beyond the few minutes they usually last. Anytime I want to, I can relive the compliment by just rereading it. This is also a good way to show appreciation for the compliments you get, because people really like the fact that you think so much of what they said that you want to preserve it. You can also pay people compliments in writing, perhaps leaving a card with an appropriate compliment on your partner's pillow.

We all can use more praise, whether we know it or not. Verbal "strokes" are part of the basic human requirements for loving connection with others. We men also like indirect compliments in the form of attention and approval paid to the women we are with. How important is this?

54. Does being with an attractive woman make you feel more attractive and successful?

"I'm actually embarrassed to say yes . . . but it does."

"Definitely!"

"It makes me feel good, and I suppose that is a part of it. It says to the world that I am an attractive man able to appeal to

a very lovely woman. It's not so important that I would continue seeing a beautiful woman who wasn't pleasing me in other ways.''

''I dated a woman who was wonderful but far from gorgeous, and I didn't have as much fun showing her off in public as I do my current love. Maybe this is petty of me, but it does give me a surge of pride when we're out together.''

''When I was very young (nineteen to twenty-two). Today I feel that way with or without a woman.''

''One of my most disappointing relationships in my twenties was with a great-looking woman, a professional dancer, who only wanted to stay home with me. I wanted to take her out dancing or to visit my friends, but she was a loner, and hardly anyone I know ever got to meet her. She didn't even like my taking pictures of her, so I only have two from the entire year together. Now, on looking back, I realize that just being with such a good-looking woman felt good, but at the time it wasn't quite enough—I wanted to have everyone out there know how lucky I was. Today, I don't think it matters as much, but I still like walking into a room and having everyone stop and stare at my date.''

About a fourth of the men interviewed answered the above question with a simple "no," and another fourth answered "yes." While the more sensitive and secure a man is, the less dependent he'll be on having a good-looking woman on his arm, every man seems to like the feeling, whether it makes him feel better about himself or not. And, a very related question:

55. How important is it to you that a woman you are with be attractive to other men?

About half the men said it wasn't very important at all. The rest of the responses varied only slightly in indicating that they would like other men to find their partner attractive.

''Seven, on a scale of one to ten.''

"It helps!"

"Not at all—but I want her to be neat, clean, and presentable in public."

"Reasonably important. In college, it was a primary considera-tion. Less so, now . . . but still there."

But what about our friends and what they think about our choices? I remember losing interest in one woman I dated in my early twenties because none of my friends liked her. In fact, they seemed repulsed by her. Looking back, they were probably right, but at the time I had been enjoying her company. I didn't give myself time to form my own opinion, but relied on theirs instead. I haven't done that in a long time, but it's still nice that my friends usually are attracted favorably to the women in my life.

56. Do your friends' opinions matter in your choice of a woman? Is it important they think she's really beautiful and wonderful?

"I don't consult my friends about my choice of women; I share my feelings with them."

"No! It's nice to get approval, but what I want from my friends is support."

"Not so much my male friends, but if one of my women friends has a strong negative reaction to a woman I'm seeing, I begin to wonder whether there's something I'm missing, especially if it's a friend who usually is enthusiastic about my choices. I realize it may be my friend's problem, or that this new woman in my life reminds them of someone they didn't like, or whatever, but it still makes me a bit uncertain about my original choice."

"Not really anymore, but they used to."

"Not in the least. I have to live with her; they don't!"

"Yes, but secondary to my opinion."

"Yes, their opinions do matter, particularly if I value their judgment."

"Yes, but then they usually agree with my opinion."

"Two of my closest friends really know me, sometimes better than I know myself. If they have a negative or so-so reaction to a woman I've introduced them to, it's usually because they've sensed some doubt in my mind about her even before I'm fully aware of it. My two friends are married to each other and have the wonderful kind of a relationship I want for myself, so I do respect their opinion . . . maybe sometimes even more than my own, since they've achieved all they each want in a love relationship, and I haven't done so yet."

There is no denying that the more we value our friends' opinions the more likely those opinions are to influence our actions and choices. These men, however, seem to have the sensible attitude that the main opinion to consider is their own, since they, after all, are experiencing the woman in question more completely than any of their friends. The one possible exception is a thirty-three-year-old college professor who has never been married but is now living with the first woman he has ever lived with.

"Arthur is my best friend; he also happens to be Lauri's ex-husband. They were married four years and split up amiably about three years ago. I started dating her about two years ago, with his permission and encouragement. I had always liked her —I knew her as his wife for the last year of their marriage—but hadn't really thought about dating her until he suggested it. I guess I thought he'd feel uncomfortable, but he's now happily married. He and his wife are good friends with Lauri, and the four of us often get together. If he had not thought she'd be really good for me, if he had had any strong feelings against my dating her, I don't think I would have bothered, and I would have missed a wonderful relationship. It does feel a bit funny when we're out together and Lauri and Arthur remember something they once did together, but they don't overdo the remembering stuff, and we all enjoy each other's company."

* * *

As couples split and regroup in small circles of camaraderie, the preceding will become more commonplace, a friend having been the former lover or spouse of someone we're interested in. As long as everyone seems comfortable with this, it can be valuable to have direct information from someone who once lived with the object of our desire . . . assuming they haven't had their opinions clouded by a lot of resentment and hostility. My personal experience in this area consists of having cordial relations with the current men in the lives of two of my ex-partners. Both men are much more suited to the specific needs of these two very special women, who were responsible for a lot of love and pleasure through six years of my life.

To close this chapter, here is perhaps one of the most telling questions of all:

57. **If you had a daughter, what would you advise her as the most important thing to do in order to have a successful love relationship?**

"Find someone it feels wonderful to be with and love and cherish him with all your heart."

"Allow your partner to be the way he is and support him totally in this."

"Be open, honest, and loving."

"Learn how to really and truly trust another human being."

"Be able to celebrate the momentary pleasures and passions, so that you will even gain from the ones that don't last."

"Just let yourself feel and don't let your logical-rational mind get in the way of what you're feeling."

"Be able to give and take and communicate."

"Work toward emotional maturity."

"Ask for what you want, and don't settle for less than you deserve."

"Always be in touch with your feelings and keep communication channels open."

"Find a man worthy of serving, then serve him well."

"Learn how to give a great massage, how to be tender and loving, how to cook a wonderful meal, how to lead an interesting and successful life . . . and don't settle for any man who can't bring into the relationship as much as you're bringing!"

This kind of "let's pretend" question often taps into some core reality within our subconscious minds. Don't you think that any of these men would be more than happy to find a woman offering exactly what they would tell their daughters to offer?

Though encumbered by the limitation of trying to use words to express feelings, the men who've responded to this survey have done an inspiring job of honest, introspective sharing. These are men who have been in relationships, are in relationships, and have learned a great deal about what they want in a loving, committed, one-to-one relationship with a woman.

What impresses me most about their answers is how often they talk about feelings rather than material desires. We men want to *feel* a certain kind of feeling before we're willing to make a real commitment. Through our collective hundreds of years of experience, we have a pretty good idea of the kind of woman, the kind of qualities, the kind of sharing that will evoke that feeling. To know us is not necessarily to love us, but to know what we want certainly brings you closer to knowing who we really are.

3

FEAR OF
FEMALE

In this chapter men talk about the things men are least likely to talk about, especially to women: their fears, doubts, confusions, anger, and vulnerability.

We men are talking about some of our gut-level reactions to the modern woman, acknowledging that women *do* frighten us at certain times with certain behaviors, attitudes, and expectations.

58. Have you been able to say to a woman in your life, "Hey, that scares me!"?

Since these men were selected for their high level of openness, I expected and got mostly "yes" answers to this question, with a few "sometimes." Only one man said this had never occurred—"*I don't remember being 'scared' by a woman. Other negative things, yes, but not frightened.*" But I happen to know this particular man, and remember quite well a period a few years ago when he and his current partner had split . . . and if that wasn't fear expressing itself in his attitude, posture, and facial expression, then he's invented a new emotion!

It takes a very stable emotional base for a man to admit to a woman that he is feeling fear. So much of our male conditioning has to do with keeping a tight rein on our feelings, the mark of courage being not to blink an eye or let out a whimper as the doctor removes the bullet. And we must *never* express any doubt whatsoever that we know exactly where we're going, what we're doing, and who we want to do it with, and be confident of complete victory every day of our lives. That's a tall order to fill, and it's no wonder so many men fall short.

Again, being human is better than being perfect. Sensitive and courageous men willing to let women know when they feel threatened, intimidated, uncertain, and frightened have found that a strong, loving woman appreciates a man with human emotions. He's someone she can relate to much more easily than the unfeeling creatures so many men have felt they had to pretend to be. For most of us men, such feelings are just beginning to see the light of day; they're still fragile, marked "handle with care." Men want gentle, whispering acceptance of these emotions by women, rather than overpowering demands for *More! More! More!*

59. What can a woman do that makes you feel threatened . . . so much so you might not ask her out even though you find her attractive?

"Be dishonest and too loud, aggressive, pushy. Be sexually involved, or nearly so with another male."

"Be very opinionated and self-righteous about anything. Possibly, too, a statement like, 'I'll bet you're great in bed' would scare the hell out of me. Any voiced expectation like that probably would."

"Act belligerent."

"Come on as very sexually experienced and arrogant, with that kind of knowing smirk that says, 'I'm more than you can handle.'"

"When she tries to take charge of me. One very attractive woman turned me off when we went to a restaurant and she grabbed my arm and led me to a table, then when the waiter asked if we were ready to order, said, 'Yes!' without consulting me. I think she would have liked me to come into her house, but I was petrified of the idea of going to bed with her. I just pictured her telling me exactly what to do—yelling out instructions—without any concern for what I wanted."

"Be overly harsh and intellectually cynical."

"Coming on very superior so you feel you can't keep pace with her."

"Yell at me. That's all it takes . . . or even tell me how she yells at others!"

"If she is too dependent."

"By telling me right away that she has children who really need a father."

"Sound as though men are after her all the time, or come across as really needy—like she may show up on my doorstep the next day, even though I may not really want to see her again."

"Push me to call her, making sure I write down her number."

"Tell me about all the wonderful places men have taken her."

Most of the responses could be summed up in one word: *pushiness.* As women grow more independent and self-supportive, they unfortunately sometimes take on some of the old male stereotypes, such as the aggressive approach. Well, women learned how to deal with this approach over many generations. Men have not had to deal with it until quite recently. An aggressive technique is great for the woman who wants to throw a man off balance, but it doesn't very often lead to warm human contact.

60. What threatens you *most* about women today?

I want to emphasis that the answers included here all come from very strong, masculine men, for the most part secure in themselves and in their relationships.

Joe is twenty-eight, has never been married, is a computer engineer living for the past three years with a woman he's known for nine years.

"The most threatening thing has to do with somehow threatening my masculinity, like implying that I don't look good enough or something like that. All sorts of performance kinds of things, including sexual performance. In the day-to-day world there's a kind of sexual evaluation going on with women you meet, as if they were saying, 'Is this person up to my sexual standards' or 'You're not up to my sexual standards.' These sorts of judgments I find threatening . . . or the fear that these judgments are going to be made, that I'm not good-looking enough, cool enough, or whatever. This would mainly be with someone I'm just meeting, but with someone I know well a threat would be much more real: a bone of contention, like marriage, where each person has a side and doesn't want to give it up and the emotional weapons come out . . . and the feeling that I may lose this and this and this if I don't give up my position. Though this is more of a real threat than judgments about my masculinity, I feel I can deal with it better, since you can always negotiate."

Pat is a forty-three-year-old commercial artist and art teacher. He was married once for six-and-a-half years, and has lived with five women, including his current relationship partner. That relationship is a year old, and they've been living together for five months. She's a dancer and dance teacher.

"Before the relationship I'm now in, the first thing that would've come to mind would have been sexuality, related to performance—that I wasn't good enough, wasn't giving her enough stimulation, couldn't last long enough . . . with the woman giving me feedback to that effect. Or even if it wasn't overtly said, it was implied. The cold shoulder. You know, the things that aren't said that say reams and volumes. I also felt threatened by my ex-wife making evaluations of my career effectiveness. Those judgments by someone who is so close to you are much more lethal than coming from a man, or even a woman you don't know well. That's all in the past. In my current relationship, I can't think of anything that threatens me."

Steve is a forty-year-old college professor and psychologist who was married once for five years, lived with three women before his current partner, whom he's known for seven years and lived with for five.

"Marriage scares me. Even when I did get married, it was after months and years of her talking about wanting to do it. I think I did it mainly to placate her rather than because I felt marriage was what I wanted. Marriage is the number-one threat. Also, for me, it's always been very difficult to tell a long-standing relationship partner that I love her. Particularly when she says, 'You haven't said that in three months,' and she's getting upset and I start feeling it's an inadequacy in me—either having a hard time saying it or not feeling it to the level that I think I should feel it in order to say it. I guess I have a high standard of what I mean when I say 'I love you'—probably unrealistically high—and this makes it hard for me to say it, because I like to be triggered when I'm actually feeling it."

* * *

Jay is an arranger and composer. He's thirty-five, has lived with five different women from one to three years, and has never been married. He isn't living with anyone right now, but is dating several women.

"One of the things I have a lot of trouble with is inarticulated demands. A woman will be taking offense at something I do or some series of things I do, and I won't know about it. I'll be going along my merry way and all of a sudden it will come out in some horrendous storm. I think it's important for me to have a woman be articulate about what's going on with her step-by-step as we go through an intimate relationship. I have a lot of trouble dealing with this, and I don't like it at all."

Josh is a forty-two-year-old writer who's never been married, lived with one woman for three years, has been unattached for the past three years, is now dating a woman five years older than he, and has an ongoing affair with a married woman who lives across the country.

"Women who come on very strong sexually sometimes threaten me, because there's a performance thing. I had one experience with a woman I'd been dating, where we made love for about two hours, and she had about six orgasms, and we started winding down, and I'm thinking it's really going to be nice to cuddle and relax in each other's arms . . . and all of a sudden she starts yelling for more, and I'm just totally spent. There's the realization that women have this biological power over us."

You might have noticed a difference in the pacing of these last five answers compared to most of those up to now. These five men were all members of a men's consciousness discussion group that discussed some of these questions, and the preceding is transcription of their response to this specific question.

Some of the other answers:

"Their independence."

"Not being liked by the ones I like."

"Expectations around the male role."

"Their sexual confidence."

"A woman wanting me to come on like a strong male figure —being a rough, tough lover, being able to fix things in the house, being good at sports . . . none of which is me. I'm good at showing a woman my good points, but not if I have to start out by defending myself because I don't meet up to her standards of what a man is."

What do these answers reveal about these men? Well, these are men highly recommended by women as sensitive and vulnerable; most of them have been very successful in their intimate relationships. The answers illustrate that these men are not scared out of the running just because sometimes a woman threatens or intimidates them. In trying to discover what these men really want from women, we can certainly see that they *don't* want to be frightened away.

The energy created between a man and a woman attracted to each other is one of the precious events in human experience. To contaminate this with any kind of threatening behavior seems the height of cynicism and self-defeatism.

In a workshop, a woman once asked me how she could reach out and touch a man without making him uncomfortable, for she was a toucher. I suggested that she approach a man as she would a newborn baby. We are oh-so-careful when reaching out to a baby. If it flinches, or expresses the slightest discomfort, we pull back. There is a part of each of us that is just as new and fragile as a baby, and it wants that same kind of tender treatment. If we *care* about making contact with a member of the opposite sex, we'll approach that person very *care*fully.

Men do seem to be put off by a very blatant sexual approach, as several of these answers indicate. Recall also the response to Question 19 in the first chapter: "Do you ever get the feeling from a very sexually open and assertive woman that she may demand too much from you in the way of sexual performance?" One of the answers to that question, not reported in the first chapter, talks about how an otherwise positive attribute in a woman can be threatening if used in a certain way.

"I love sexually open and assertive women, so it all has to do with the way they put that out. If it comes across as rough and strident, I assume they are not really at home with their sexuality, but are trying to control me in some way. With the soft and gentle approach, I can just relax, and the woman can be just as open and just as forthright. I like a large dose of 'femininity' with my sex."

Many men used to say that all they wanted was a sexually free and available woman, but that was when women were more reserved and less available. Now when women use their sexuality in nonloving ways, men respond nonlovingly.

When I was eleven or twelve, someone—I think it was an aunt or uncle—gave me a prescription for happiness that I haven't thought about in nearly thirty years; it only recently popped up from my memory banks. It was, simply: "Find a good woman and treat her right." I do hope I've lived by it. I don't think it made much sense to me the first time I heard it—certainly not as much as it does in the context of the responses of 101 sensitive men.

We all just want to find a good partner and treat him or her right and be treated right in return. If this sounds simplistic, so be it. In a conversation with noted anthropologist Ashley Montagu some years ago, he said that when solutions are found to the major human problems, they will *all* be simple ones.

61. **Are you ever threatened by a woman who seems so self-sufficient that she really doesn't need a man around?**

Sensitive men don't want a woman who "needs" a man, but rather one who wants and enjoys a man, so the overwhelming response to this question was "No."

62. **Do you ever find yourself intimidated or scared off by an exceptionally beautiful woman?**

Some 75 percent of the men said they sometimes were.

"Yes, but I'm getting over it."

"Yes. I rationalize and say that because she's pretty she never had to get her act together otherwise—which is only true sometimes."

"Once, when one remarked that she couldn't find a man who could satisfy her sexually."

"It makes me cautious. I feel she's generally been spoiled by males and not worth having."

Most men believe, at some deep level, that somehow a beautiful woman is different inside from other women, that somehow her awareness of her own beauty provides her with a tougher outer shell, a supreme confidence, and less need for attention and affection from mere mortals.

Since self-esteem is an emotional quality, not a physiological one, nothing could be further from reality. While some beautiful women have had their self-image reinforced and supported by other people's praise and appreciation, just as many haven't. They don't really believe the compliments they get. I am constantly being surprised by beautiful women who are just as shy, just as unsure of themselves as the most unappealing physical specimen. For me, coming from a very shy and late-blooming youth, a major breakthrough in my life was the discovery that beautiful women are just as approachable and available as anyone else—sometimes more so, because everyone else has assumed they're not. Perhaps this is why, of all the answers to this question, my favorite is *"I was always a bit afraid of a really beautiful woman . . . until I married one!"*

This statement illustrates one of the affirmations I teach in my workshops: *Action diminishes fear.* If we allow fear to immobilize us, we merely feed and perpetuate it. If we move forward, the fear almost magically starts fading away. It is a testimonial to the fact that here we have very special men, men who can admit their fears and doubts and go on to make their relationships work. And I imagine that the women in their lives have acquired a certain talent for creating a safety zone where the man can express what he doesn't want as well as what he does. A lot of men said they would join me in saying that what I really want from a woman is someone I can turn to in my joy and just as easily in my pain or fear, knowing that she will share in the one and kiss away my fears in the other.

For many people, confusion and uncertainty are the most frightening emotions of all.

63. Are you attracted or repulsed by a woman who seems uncertain of herself and what she wants out of life?

I asked this question because this used to be a major problem in my own relationships. A woman who expressed her confusion to me reminded me too much of my own. That was something I wanted to avoid. As I grew more secure about myself and what I wanted, I became more willing to see confusion as an inherent part of all our lives. We always seem to avoid people who remind us of what we want to avoid in ourselves.

But there are two kinds of confusion—that experienced by someone trying to decide among a number of healthy choices and that of someone who can't find a single viable alternative. The former someone *can* be a nourishing, supportive love partner; the latter probably can't. Men, at least the men interviewed here, seem to prefer a woman who is sure of herself and knows what she wants most of the time.

"Somewhat repulsed, but not always."

"It can turn me off, unless she has so much else going for her that it overshadows her doubts."

"It really depends. Not knowing what one wants out of life can be a creative and exciting place full of potential. I think it's those people who deal with the situation by feeling lost or depressed that I avoid."

"If she's at a crossroads, that's O.K. But if she isn't interested in truly growing and wishes just to latch on to a man for security, I'm not attracted."

"There have been times that I've been very attracted to a woman and found that her confusion kept her from being able to either give or receive love. In that sense, I was repulsed. If someone can't be present for me, then I tend to go AWOL."

64. What confuses you most about women today?

"With some, it's their immaturity and disorganization."

"Crossed messages between 'strength' and 'sensitivity,' between 'freedom' and 'responsibility,' between 'flexibility' and 'commitment.'"

"Why so many fight their inner nature to love and serve their man."

"Their expectations."

"Their lack of sensitivity—in some aspects they are becoming more like men used to be with regard to feelings."

"When and how to come on, and who makes the first move."

"Their emotions."

"Why a woman will claim to want to hear about what I'm

really feeling, and then when I tell her she uses it against me."

"When they're contrary."

"Their roles used to be so much more clearly defined. I would meet a very sweet, soft-spoken woman and would know she was shy and that I had to be very gentle with her. Now she's just as likely to rip my clothes off, while some women who dress very sexy and talk to match are only available to a man who will live with or marry them. I wish they would wear labels!"

It seems most of the men questioned want more clarity from women. Perhaps some communication is needed in this area as our roles expand. Perhaps we should ask each other outright, "What do you want from me as a man/woman in your life?" And after each partner has answered the question, both might respond to a followup question: "What expectations of what a member of the opposite sex would do for you and add to your life do I not seem to be fulfilling for you?"

The dramatic changes of the last twenty years have confused all of us to some degree, and some sharing of feelings about this can help to clear out all the emotional distractions connected with role expectations.

I once dated a lovely woman over a period of three months, to whom I one day suggested that I might buy some ingredients for a gourmet dinner that she could then cook with my assistance. She was afraid to tell me that she had no cooking skills, hated the idea of cooking, wouldn't even enjoy visiting with me in the kitchen while I cooked! Like all men now in their forties, I was brought up in an era when women cooked a hot meal every night for their men, and this was a reasonable expectation at the time. At some subliminal level it's still an expectation—we can never completely erase our early conditioning. But if I meet a woman and she tells me she doesn't like to cook right at the beginning, I immediately confront and modify that role expectation, so that we go out to eat or I do the cooking. It's not very hard to make the shift if I get the right information. And if, as has been true in several love relationships, she adores expressing her creativity by cooking, I just relax and enjoy it.

I wouldn't be surprised if, on further probing, we found that some of the men who, in Question 15 in Chapter 1, chose a romantic restaurant did so because they wouldn't feel comfortable suggesting that a woman cook for them on the first date. First they'd want to know her feelings about cooking and acting out the "traditional" female role of cooking for a man. It's such a touchy and ambiguous area nowadays that a lot of men would just as soon avoid any confrontation on this issue at the beginning of a relationship.

I personally get a lot of joy out of preparing food for a woman; I don't expect a woman to cook for me if she's not getting the same kind of pleasure out of it. On the other hand, I don't want a woman taking it for granted that I'm going to cook for her every time we're together. It's enjoyable as a once-in-a-while treat, a gift to give someone I care about. Most women I've talked to on this subject feel the same way—they never want to get back into the old role of the woman having to come up with at least one meal a day, whether she works or not, whether she's tired or not, whether she wants to or not!

More on this as we explore the effect of the women's movement and the emergence of new liberated woman on men's desires, feelings, and fears, later in this chapter.

65. What confuses you most about your own role in a relationship?

"Why it isn't easier."

"Sex. I'm not sure I'm supposed to always make the first move,

or whether it's O.K. to just let her 'have her way with me,' which she seems to enjoy."

"Tenderness and vulnerability . . . when it's appropriate and when it's not, when it's safe and when it's not."

"What kind of commitment to make to get what I want for myself."

"How to respond when a woman comes on to me. It's pleasant and flattering as hell, but I just don't know what my next step is supposed to be."

"My own feelings . . . and not always knowing what they are so that I can discuss them with my partner."

"What a woman wants from me."

"My feelings of jealousy and possessiveness."

"I'm not sure when I'm being selfish in a negative way, as compared to when I am just being strong and looking out for my needs in a positive manner."

It's a lot of work to pretend you are confident when you're not, to pretend you have clear goals and a sense of direction when you are confused. In discussions with some of the men interviewed—and with many others who've attended my workshops over the years—what comes across is that men are tired of holding on to the old role of the man without a doubt in his mind as to what he wants and where he is going. The reason they do pretend is that they believe this is the kind of man a woman wants. In admitting their confusion, the sensitive and confident men in this survey have discovered that most women are drawn to a man with these doubts . . . as long as he doesn't hide them behind a Rock of Gibraltar exterior and as long as they aren't the major focus of his life.

In the dating/mating ritual, we are so accustomed to using guile and subterfuge to get what we want that it takes a real effort of will to open up about our doubts. One of the things I want for myself in a relationship is a nurturing and compassionate woman. When I open up about my own confusion, these are the precise traits of a woman that get triggered into response. But even knowing this, it isn't always easy. For men are still learning to emerge from the cocoon they've built for themselves, still finding out that they *can* get more of what they want by being more of who they are.

66. What do you want a woman to know about you that you might not feel comfortable telling?

"That I have both a strong and a weak, fearful side . . . that there are still sexual inhibitions that are a part of my past that I'm growing out of . . . and that I feel I'm basically a neat person."

"Things I'm proud of about myself."

"That I'm turned on to her."

"My track record."

"That I have a lot of feelings."

"That I'm a very spiritual person."

"That I'm battling insecurity in some aspects of my life."

"That I have a lot of personal debts and am in no position to assume any financial responsibility for another person."

"That I love God. The whole spiritual area is hard to talk about."

The last comment is from a forty-nine-year-old family therapist and minister. He's had three marriages and says, *"I am currently and conclusively married . . . and have been for seven years."* I mention this because I find it interesting that several men said they felt uncomfortable talking about their religious devotion. Also, I just love the purpose and commitment evident in a term I've never heard used before: *conclusively married.*

"I enjoy a lot of sex."

"That, though I'm a very successful sex therapist, I still am

not completely at ease with my own sexuality. "

"That I've slept with over five hundred women in the past twenty years."

"I have never, ever been able to tell a woman, even my ex-wife, that I had a homosexual relationship as a teenager that lasted two years."

"Once, ten years ago in an intensive therapy workshop, and here now, anonymously though, I can admit that I was arrested three times for shoplifting in my late teens. I guess I haven't felt safe enough in any of my relationships to share that."

"There was no way I could tell my last partner that I found her sagging breasts very unappealing, and got completely turned off whenever she asked me to play with them or suck her nipples. Our sex life was a disaster, and I even thought of paying for cosmetic surgery, but I couldn't talk about it with her."

Even among these men, much more willing to open up than the general male population, 80 percent had at least one thing they were uncomfortable telling, sometimes *very* uncomfortable. And yet these are things they would *want* the woman to know about them.

Perhaps one thing women can learn from this is that they still have some distance to go in making it completely safe for a man to reveal himself, *if* they really want him to share his deepest secrets.

And one thing we men are going to have to learn is how to let a woman know that she hasn't made it safe enough for us yet, not if she wants to hear it all.

67. **One of the things that women say they hate most is a man who withdraws or runs away as soon as they seem to be getting close. Have you ever done that? What triggered it?**

This is one of a number of questions specifically suggested by what women have told me *they* want and don't want in a relationship. Of all the things they don't want, of all the things a man can do to hurt, anger, frustrate, or confuse them, this is the biggest, the one that creates the most emotional pain for them. And it ranges from a man just putting up a slight wall, where he doesn't seem quite as open as before, to his actually disappearing from her life without writing or calling—without explaining his reasons. When I confronted men on this, three quarters admitted that they had been guilty of this type of withdrawal.

A lot of the women I talked to said they were going to read this book *just* to get the answers to this question, so here they are:

"Yes. Lack of mutual depth of feeling as well as a general sense of not being ready for that kind of commitment."

"Yes. I was afraid of being rejected if she really knew me."

"When getting close really means she is desperately seeking my approval, I withdraw. That puppydog, 'pat me on the head' look causes me to withdraw every time."

"Yes. Feeling too much emotion. It's hard for me to handle."

"Yes. Not ready for commitment. Women too possessive too quickly."

"Yes, I have. Sometimes it was a sense I was being smothered; other times I was too scared to get close."

"I used to a lot. It's triggered by unspoken demands (real or imagined), too much togetherness, crowding on her part encouraged by me."

"Yes. Felt I was getting smothered. No room for my own identity."

Since this is such a crucial issue, I brought it up at the men's consciousness discussion group mentioned at the beginning of this chapter.

Pat: *"Pressing for an involvement that I don't want or that I'm not ready to get into . . . and that is one of the easiest ways in the world for me to turn off in a relationship, to go away from the thing. With some women, it seems that if you are open or show some vulnerability, they interpret that to mean 'Move in' or 'Let's get real close.' It's like overkill, and I back out of the relationship. It can just be that you felt open and vulnerable at that moment and you really don't want to spend the rest of your life with them."*

Jay: *"I think it's a question of one person who wants more out of the relationship than the other person . . . and I can think of one relationship where that was true for the woman. And because I didn't want as much out of it as she did, she perceived me as being withdrawn. But I just didn't want to be more involved with her. I think if both people want to be as intimate with each other, then that doesn't come up. If one wants more intimacy than the other is willing to give, then they are going to see that other person as closing down."*

Steve: *"I think women have been trained and are capable of a lot more intimacy, and once they see somebody they like, it's immediately 'Close in' and 'I want it!' while we males have been trained that intimacy is just one aspect of our lives, and our work is another. I generally see men as not wanting to jump in as quickly, and intimacy is definitely one of the major male fears. I think it's endemic. I find myself closing off especially if a woman starts talking about marriage and I'm not ready for it."*

Jay: *"I think I have a fear of intimacy, especially intimacy too quickly. I have to really get to know someone and to be comfortable with them. Another thing I've experienced is feeling I know a woman and feeling like getting closer . . . and then suddenly I look to her like the answer to her prayers, and then it's bye-bye time. I usually withdraw rather than saying, 'Hey, I don't like the way things are going!'—sort of sneaking out the back."*

Steve: *"I think it's much more common for men to feel entrapment and women abandonment."*

Joe: *"If they're too forward with their demands that I be more sharing or vulnerable, I tend to shut off."*

Josh: *"I'm getting much better than I used to be on this issue. In the past, when a woman seemed to be moving in—clasping me to her bosom, so to speak, and just assuming that we were an irreversible item—I would panic. I couldn't begin to share these fears and feelings with the woman, believing it would destroy her or totally eliminate her from my life. So what I did, time after time, was start to shut down the furnace, start to close off my feelings. If I felt tender or loving toward her, I wouldn't tell her, for fear she'd get even more convinced that we were made for each other. What finally made the difference for me was the realization that she had no power over me that I didn't want to give her, that I could leave at any time, that there was no point of no return. Now, I'll share those feelings with a woman I care about. I'll tell her if I feel we're getting too close too fast. But there's still a part of me that gets frightened as intimacy builds. Sharing those fears gets me much more of what I want than I used to get when I was into running away."*

When a group of men who are described by women as "willing to be open and vulnerable" still express fears of intimacy, I see it as a powerful message that we men still have a lot of growing to do in that area. And we can't do it without the help of women. It appears that one of the hardest things for a man to say is, "I'm not as involved with you emotionally as you say you are with me." We don't want to hurt a woman's feelings, and maybe we're just a bit embarrassed and/or guilty that we aren't loving them as much as they seem to be loving us. I think it's significant that a lot of the men responding used the word *smother* in describing the pressure they feel from a woman to get closer.

One of the interesting facets of this issue—mentioned

by Pat in the men's encounter group—is that some women interpret vulnerability on the part of a man as a signal to intensify or deepen the relationship. There's a feeling among men that all we have to say is, "I want to share some feelings with you," and she's going to respond with, "Wow! Let's get married!" Maybe it's an unrealistic fear on our part, but it is based on the reality that some women confuse our vulnerability, our feeling of safety with them, with a desire for more commitment on our part. It's difficult enough for a man just to begin to show himself to a woman. It only makes it more difficult when she interprets that first gentle dipping of feet in the water as an unspoken declaration of love and lifetime devotion.

As I begin to share myself more deeply with a woman, I may or may not want to enter into a deeper commitment. One is not synonymous with the other, though they may occur simultaneously. Again, preconceived notions and unstated assumptions cause a lot of the basic misunderstandings in relationships.

I am not trying to excuse our cowardice in running away, but understanding our reasons for doing so can create some new insight into a major obstacle to male/female communication. Since many of the things men think, feel, and do are totally foreign to women, and vice versa, creating understanding between the sexes often requires the same diplomatic care as between two foreign governments.

The main reason anyone runs away from anything is fear. Unexpressed fear feeds on itself. We men are going to have to be more willing to tell a woman what we're afraid of. Women are going to have to create an environment of trust and acceptance so that we feel safer doing that.

As I talked about this issue with the men's encounter

group, I wondered aloud about another possible reason men so often withdraw or run away:

"Do you think it might have something to do with the fact that we men realize women are better at intimacy than we are, more into their feelings? When it gets to a feeling level of communicating, do men get scared off because they realize they're having a confrontation in an area in which women are superior . . . sort of a case of retreating from the battlefield when faced with a superior army, one more experienced and better equipped? Especially when women are pushy about it—'Why don't you get into your feelings?' etc.—when men would much rather be gently brought along in this area."

Pat: *"I think for most men it is frightening as hell to have to think about, deal with, or list their 'Oh, my God!' emotions. There are things in me that are just like a woman, that can break down and be sobbing and hysterical, in wanting someone to comfort me and pamper me and take care of me and just tell me it's O.K. That's like opening up the jaws of hell for some men— it's like total insanity, total out-of-controlness—so no wonder they run away from feelings like that. For me, as far as a woman confronting me about being more emotional, it's like, 'Hey look, give me a break, lady. You've been brought up to be an emotional mushball. I haven't. You've been brought up where it's O.K. to break down and cry; it's O.K. to have tears running down your face in a movie.' She's been given an emotional license for free expression. I wasn't."*

Steve: *"Most of us men will turn to a woman to be understood, to be listened to. Most of us will turn to a woman to hear us out, to really feel we're understood. And most women will also turn to a woman for this."*

Pat: *"A difference in training and background is what I see. They have more experience . . . if you're talking about being empathetic, being understanding, listening to someone's feelings* and being more compassionate and all of that. Those are the kinds of emotional, soft things we associate with females. Those are the kinds of things they've been taught. They've been taught to be nice and loving and warm. We were taught to go out and perform, achieve, and be nonemotional, competent, rational, and maintain control."

Steve: "I think men have more trouble sharing their doubts and fears. Men have tremendous trouble saying, 'I just don't know,' sharing their inadequacies. Ninety-five percent of the time when a man gets upset he feels angry. When a woman gets upset, she feels hurt, vulnerable; she's afraid. A man tends to push you away when threatened, not let you see his inner core."

Josh: "True, and nothing gets me angrier than a woman insisting that I must feel hurt or angry when I don't feel it, or at least am not in touch with it."

Another aspect of this issue is expressed by Warren Farrell, Ph.D., author of *The Liberated Man,* who conducts a very popular workshop entitled "Why Men Are the Way They Are," in which every woman in the audience gets to play out male roles in various experiences. As Dr. Farrell sees it, men often end up overpromising intimacy as a result of the setting up of certain conditions by women. As he told me:

"Women are almost invariably more conditional about their sexuality and require some type of emotional involvement from the man as a condition for being open sexually. Men, in order to shorten the period between meeting the woman and sexual intimacy, have learned to promise or suggest that this emotional involvement is there. The man thus ends up trying to provide the conditions the woman requires, and the reason he does this is to shorten the period of potential rejection. Because the more he tells her, 'I care for you; you're special,' that sort of thing, and opens up and is vulnerable, the more he believes she will be more sexually responsive to him, and thus his period of potential sexual rejection will be lessened. So, having overpromised his intimacy and his desire for her on a long-term level, sexual intimacy has occurred. The woman is often operating on the assumption that he meant everything he said. And he starts reassessing: Did he mean everything he said? Sort of backing off and not wanting to get committed on the level that he was sort of promising and on the level that the woman is escalating it to. It's not only the man saying it, but the woman usually escalates it beyond that."

The men in this group seem to think women are better at feelings than men, so I asked this question in the survey:

68. **Do you think women are more in touch with and better at expressing feelings than men?**
"Generally, yes."
"Yes, but I find that sometimes women turn me off by acting superior about this."
"Definitely. But I feel I am a rare male in that I'm trying to be in touch with my feelings, and this gives me an advantage in relating to women over most other men."
"Yes, it seems to be more natural for them."
"In general, yes. To me, no."
"No, not naturally—they were just raised to do that. They are just people, not superior."

Without exception, all of the men feel women are more comfortable with and better at expressing emotions than most men.

Another obvious question raised in this area is:

69. **Do you ever feel pushed upon to share your feelings by a woman, when you're not really ready to do so?**

"Only when I am tired."

"At times."

"Not really."

"No, I'm easy that way."

"Yes, my feelings are often not as strong or clear as hers seem to be. I have had to learn they are just as valid."

"Not anymore. It's usually the other way around."

A lot of men echoed the last comment, saying that this might have been true when they were younger and less able to express their feelings, but it doesn't happen anymore. Eighty-eight percent of the men said "No" to this question, indicating that they either feel much better sharing their feelings when a woman wants them to do so, or that they are choosing women who don't push them on this issue. Perhaps both are true for these men.

In terms of valuable information women can gather for themselves on this particular subject, the most pertinent question of all might be:

70. **What can a woman say or do that allows you most easily to open up and show your tender, vulnerable side?**

"Be sensitive—ask me about me and share about herself. Ask for my help with an emotional problem. This always brings out the tenderness in men."

"Listen without criticism or judgment."

"Accept me. If there is need or demand, I get guarded. It happens best when we are tender and vulnerable together."

"When she is honest and open, sensitive and loving."

"Mostly come across that she's strong and loving enough to want to really know me and that she won't be easily offended or hurt by what I say or do."

"Ask me how I'm feeling and touch me."

"Be there for me and not be scared if I open up easily."

"Be open and supportive and feeling."

"Caress me and say, 'Let's talk about it.'"
"Trust me unconditionally."
"Not make it a contest of who can spill our guts the easiest."
"Let me choose my own time and place for sharing . . . and just hold me."

Gentle treatment, including a gentle touch, is what most men want in order to feel comfortable opening up. I like the comment about not making it a contest, since men and women so often try to take advantage of each other in areas in which they might be stronger or more comfortable.

All of the men wanted the woman to approach them with tenderness and acceptance, so I wondered if they are able to directly ask for this. Not necessarily. In fact, four out of every ten men questioned said "No" when I asked the following:

71. **Could you see yourself beginning the following sentence to a woman? If so, finish it.**

    "PLEASE TREAT ME GENTLY, BECAUSE I ____"

    ". . . am sensitive."
    ". . . deserve it."
    ". . . am frail."
    ". . . am emotionally sensitive in that area, and I get hurt easily. Because that is a place where I am very defensive, and I react."
    ". . . am delicate."
    ". . . would like to treat you tenderly."
    ". . . still tend to take too many things personally."

There were lots more "I'm sensitive" and "I deserve it" answers. I think the biggest revelation here is that 40 percent of the men couldn't bring themselves to ask a woman for the gentle treatment they say they want in order to be tender and vulnerable. And these are highly communicative men! This may be telling women that, if they want men to be vulnerable, they should see the man needing gentle treatment as an unspoken request.

The image has always been that women are fragile, have feelings that can easily be crushed or bruised, while men are strong and impervious to such "emotionalism." The results of this information and feeling gathering expedition show clearly that men may feel just as strongly as women but are less able to talk about it and sometimes tend to hide it even from themselves. As men become more sensitive and vulnerable, and as women become more nurturing of this aspect of their masculinity, we will all have more permission to articulate our inner experience to one another.

72. How can a woman most easily hurt your feelings?

"By assuming that I don't have any, that I'm a rock."

"By putting me down sexually."

"Rejection."

"By being sexually unfaithful."

"By being angry at me."

"Saying I'm a lousy lover or that there's nothing to respect about me."

"By expressing anger toward me when I am not really doing anything to make them angry—I just happen to be there."

"By blowing hot and cold—being warm to me one day, aloof the next."

"Break commitments."

"Be critical of my principles."

"Personal attacks on me."

"Blaming or accusing me."

73. Do you have problems handling moodiness on the part of a woman?

This seems to be a basic male complaint, that women are *too* emotional. A woman's changing moods can irritate and antagonize a man. Do *these* men, more in tune with their own emotional natures, also get turned off by a woman's "moodiness"? Some of them do.

"Some. Invariably it is when I am not centered and I either take her moods personally or try to make everything all right."

"Some problems, especially when it seems like an overall pattern."

"Yes. It's hard to know what mood they're in and hence how to react or how to act toward them."

"Yes, I tend to want to solve things for her. I feel it must mean something about me if she is not happy."

"Only if she won't communicate."

"I usually choose women who are not moody, who don't go around feeling sad or angry unless something really unpleasant has happened . . . and I don't see that as moodiness, just being alive."

The last statement points out one of the issues here. What seems to turn men off is women who create emotional responses for themselves that have nothing to do with what is going on in their life. Men can understand why a woman might be upset if she has a setback in her career, a day filled with hassles, or an argument with her mother. What they find difficult to deal with is lots of emotional ups and downs when none of these things are happening—emotions with no visible means of support, nothing to trigger them, other than some unexpressed inner turmoil. This scares men. It terrifies them in themselves, and it scares them or pushes them away from a woman.

When I was in my early twenties, I just didn't want to deal with anyone's emotions, including my own. I was dating a very sweet and sensitive woman who had a lot of deep and intense feelings. I did not feel these were acceptable, and so she shut them off from me. This cut off a lot of the energy in our relationship, which died a slow, lingering death. About six years later, I came upon some of the poetry she had written me. I started to read it and was deeply and painfully moved to see what she had been trying to say to me all along—feelings I didn't know she had because I wouldn't let her share them, feelings I had never seen when I originally read the poems. I missed a very rare opportunity to experience a very loving and vulnerable woman, because her emotions and her "moodiness" turned me off. At the time, my top priority in what I wanted from a woman was emotional consistency. Every man has certain emotional criteria, a certain way he wants a woman to be with her feelings.

74. What kind of emotional condition do you prefer in a potential love partner?

"Intensity. I enjoy intense emotional relationships."

"Excited. Receptive. Loving."

"Happy and self-sufficient. Horny is also nice."

"Well-balanced, adjusted."

"Stable and easygoing."

"Emotions under control."

"Open, responsive, loving."

"I appreciate a woman who is calm, relaxed, comfortable with herself, who doesn't repress her feelings, good or bad."

"Stable. I prefer cheerfulness and someone who responds to my romantic nature."

Whatever the reality, men believe that women are moodier than they are, and less stable emotionally. Therefore, if a woman wants a man to feel free to respond to her in loving ways, she may want to set his mind at ease on this issue.

When we get down to basics, all relationships involve two people selling themselves to each other, marketing their advantages and benefits. In any kind of sales/marketing effort, one of the first steps is overcoming any objections. If one of the major objections men have to forming a close relationship with a woman is their fear that she is moody or unstable emotionally, this objection has to be overcome before the woman can communicate all her benefits.

You might think it useful here to look at the difference between real fears and imagined fears. The problem with this is that there *is* no difference, at least not in terms of our emotional response to those fears. What a lot of people do in a relationship is try to overcome their partner's fantasy fears by telling them that these fears are unrealistic, have no basis in fact, are nothing to worry about. This, of course, misses the point entirely.

If I believe that a woman is more likely to have wide-ranging emotional changes, swift shifts in mood, and can more easily get upset, hurt, or angry, then my belief will cause me to take actions that might prevent intimacy and commitment. The only way a woman can reassure me on this is by creating a communications channel so that I recognize this belief, share it with her, and check it out against the reality of her emotional state. If she becomes defensive, as so many women do when a man just whispers the word *moody,* and starts trying to convince him that he's wrong, then he'll close up.

We are often condemned by "appearances" that reinforce other people's fears and false beliefs. For example, though we all go through emotional turmoil in our lives, let a politican admit he or she sought professional psychological help during a period of emotional stress, and a career goes down the tubes. As one woman told me:

"We're damned if we do and damned if we don't. If a woman keeps a tight rein on her feelings, she's considered a cold, unfeeling bitch, maybe even a lesbian. As soon as she shows she has feelings and is healthy enough to express them when they happen, she's another 'emotional' female, unstable and moody. I don't think it's going to change until men really believe feelings are O.K.—O.K. to have, O.K. to talk about. Even the most liberated male will run away from an emotional scene as if it were an invasion from a huge horde of foreign barbarians. And for men, feelings are still somewhat foreign, still something to be feared."

Neither side has much to gain from running away on this issue. It's getting better. The 101 men interviewed here are more willing to accept feelings in themselves and others, less likely to bolt at the first sign of a tear or a trembling lip. And the women they've chosen to be with are more willing to teach them by example that it is healthy to have and to express feelings in a relationship, that emotional intensity can make a person more interesting and more loving. It makes more sense and brings more satisfying results to view relationships as partnerships in understanding and discovery rather than as confrontations between adversaries.

75. What do you most often avoid discussing in a relationship?

Both women and men agree that men more often avoid confronting issues in a relationship. Again, it's our training to keep things to ourselves, to protect the fort by maintaining a firm defense and not admitting "weakness" or fear.

"My sexual interest in my partner."

"I avoid discussing jealousy, mine or hers."

"How much I love her . . . sometimes I just don't know, and I want time to think about it without being pressured."

"Marriage."

"Marriage. I've never been married, because I always get turned off when a woman brings it up, when it hasn't yet dawned on me that I want to spend the rest of my life with this woman . . . and her trying to discuss it convinces me that I don't"

"I never discuss my fears—what I'm afraid of in my career, what I'm sometimes afraid of from her."

"Feelings about my son."

This last is from a forty-year-old man who is married to his second wife, with whom he's just had a baby girl, while his preteen son lives with his ex-wife. Several men reported that they didn't discuss children by a former marriage with their current mate, either because of feelings of guilt over not being totally there for that child or those children or because there was a lot of pain connected with giving up custody, rather than any feeling that the new woman in their lives wouldn't understand.

A fair number of the men said they avoided discussing marriage and/or commitment—about 20 percent of them, in fact. Almost the same number avoided discussing negative feelings they or their partner had about the other. One of the most "typical" answers, however, was, *"I don't tend to bring up sex or more emotional matters related to our relationship, although I'm realizing these days the need for me to do more of that."*

Just by admitting that they *do* avoid talking about certain things, these men are being more open than most. They are aware of their deficiencies in this area. Eighty-five percent of the men said they avoided discussing at least one thing in their relationships.

76. **Do you ever feel a woman tries to take advantage of you by discussing serious issues when you are very tired or after a passionate lovemaking session?**

Nine out of ten men answered "no" to this one.

I asked this question because this used to be a favorite excuse of mine to avoid discussing something I didn't want to discuss. I say "excuse" because, though I do feel that is a particularly vulnerable time to ask someone to discuss something difficult, I rarely made the effort to set a more desirable time. Though some of the men said this was sometimes true, we have mostly gotten to a point where we're less inclined to blame women for wanting to discuss things at an inconvenient time. We can honestly tell them we're uncomfortable discussing a particular subject. And for this group of men, there is much more willingness to plunge ahead and discuss things, no matter how uncomfortable.

And that brings us to the next question:

77. When do you *prefer* to discuss issues concerning your relationship?

"Actually, it would be more in the morning, when I'm fresh, when the birds are out and we can sit in the sun and talk."

"When they arise."

"An hour or so before bedtime."

"When they come up."

"Almost any time except when I'm tired."

"Early evening or weekends, when I have time and I'm not rushing."

"Anytime, except during orgasm."

"In the morning."

"As soon as they arise."

"At dinner."

"Anytime, as long as we can do it in each other's arms."

These men *don't* feel their women try to take advantage of them by discussing issues at inappropriate times, but they *do* have favorite times to discuss important emotional and relationship matters. Although one fourth of the men said they wanted to discuss issues as they came up, the rest indicated they would still prefer choosing the time and place.

In counseling couples, I have often suggested that they agree, before crucial issues come up, on a special time set aside at least once a week for discussing whatever is bothering either partner about anything. Providing a minimal structure for such communication precludes one or the other person building a lot of resentment/hostility because no appropriate or convenient time seems to present itself for this sharing. Women seem to be better at discussing emotionally charged issues and so *do* have an advantage over men in this area. They can either press that advantage and win a lot of small "victories," or be accepting and loving about male difficulties here and win the relationship.

78. What do you find it most difficult to ask from a woman?

79. What do you find it most difficult to give a woman?

Though these are two separate questions, they are very much related; I didn't know how much until I saw how often the two separate responses connected, sometimes in very profound ways.

"(78) *To be left alone, because there are things I'd like to do.* (79) *Undevoted attention to the degree she is often looking for.*"

"(78) *Help.* (79) *To listen and be sensitive.*"

"(78) *To share my interests. I don't want to impose my value system on her.* (79) *Sharing all her interests. I don't like to have anyone impose their value system on me.*"

"(78) *Sex.* (79) *Sexual endurance.*"

"(78) *Space.* (79) *Any control over me.*"

"(78) *To pay her way.* (79) *Commitment.*"

"(78) *To be alone.* (79) *Time.*"

"(78) *Solitude. It has always been difficult to express the need to be alone, especially when she wants to be together.* (79) *Simple attention. I seem to be afraid of being bored or something. My mind wanders; I have impulses to watch TV or read . . . unless the conversation is exciting.*"

"(78) *That she pay her own way or support herself.* (79) *Lots of emotional feelings.*"

"(78) *Sex.* (79) *Affectionate touches when I'm not emotionally ready.*"

"(78) *That she touch me when she isn't doing so. I feel embarrassed even in an intimate relationship, a feeling that she would be touching me if she wanted to be, that she'd only begrudgingly do it if I asked for it.* (79) *To really be interested in what she's saying, especially if I have something going on in my mind that's more interesting to me.*"

The men found it most difficult to *ask for* sex, time alone, and that the woman pay her own way. They found it most difficult to *give* time, attention, commitment, and feelings.

These answers fascinated me, so I went back and talked to some of the men responding. "What is the most difficult thing for you to tell a woman?" I asked them. Most of them said that they found it impossible to tell a woman when she was boring them, when what she was saying held no interest whatsoever for them. The only other response that came up several times was telling the woman that she left something to be desired as a sexual partner.

I would guess that women have very similar answers to the same question. We *do* bore each other. We tend to feel that in order to be a loving relationship partner, we have to be willing to listen to whatever our partner is saying without letting our minds wander, without yawning. Otherwise we are not being empathetic; otherwise we are that most offensive of all modern psychological villains, the bad listener.

But is it really healthy to force ourselves to listen to stuff we don't feel like hearing, just because we're there? Is it really serving another person to let him or her drone on and on without saying how uninteresting it all is? In one relationship I had, my partner and I had an agreement. We would each listen for at least five minutes to whatever the other had to say, and then stop and honestly tell the person speaking whether we were interested in hearing any more. We very quickly learned what the other person most enjoyed hearing about, what held the attention. We also learned to communicate our ideas and feelings more effectively in a shorter amount of time. If someone loves me, it doesn't mean I have the right to bore her or to expect her to listen patiently no matter what I'm saying. I can get a tape recorder to do that.

80. What does a woman say or do that most often triggers a response of anger in you?

"Infidelity and drunkenness are totally unacceptable."

" 'Why don't you want to spend more time with me?' "

" 'Don't do that!' "

"Being late or other types of irresponsibility."

"When she says I'm lying and I'm not."

"It is not content that bothers me, but style. I get hurt or angry when I am attacked or blamed and I feel she is not willing to share the responsibility."

"Accuse me of being uncaring or unfeeling."

"Usually something to do with the way we raise our children."

"I get most angry when she thinks she knows more than I do about what's motivating me to do a certain thing. Maybe I just am not feeling like talking, and she insists I'm upset with her or have some deep psychological problem eating away at me."

* * *

The problem with these anger triggers is that they don't often get communicated to the person doing the triggering, especially since men so often hide their anger from women, assuming they can't handle it. If I can choose a quiet moment to tell a love partner that something she says or does triggers anger in me, then she has valuable information. If what she does or says is important for her to continue doing or saying, then we can figure out a way in which to modify or eliminate the cycle of her doing/saying it, my getting angry, her doing/saying it again, etc. If it's *not* important for her to keep doing this or saying this in my presence, then we've resolved the whole thing. It isn't always *easy* to communicate these triggers, but it is *simple* and usually worth the effort in terms of relationship benefits.

81. Does anything a woman does make you feel victimized?

This one really pushed some buttons! One fourth of the men didn't answer it at all, several going out of their way to let me know they didn't like the question. Another fourth came up with answers like this:

"No. I can't think of anything offhand. I don't accept guilt from them and if they have some behavioral problem, it's theirs, not mine."

"I would have to choose to feel victimized, it has nothing to do with the woman."

I certainly have to agree that we choose to play the role of a victim, in a relationship or in any other situation. I asked the question because so many women today are talking about men victimizing *them* that I wanted to see if men felt the reverse was true. Not as strongly, but about half the men did find something that made them feel victimized.

* * *

"Sexual come-ons until I show interest, then a turn-off."

"Dating me to fill a void after she broke off a relationship with someone else, and then going back with that person and telling me how sorry she is."

"When a woman is frequently or chronically dissatisfied or feels needy, I tend to get drawn in to feeling helpful or responsible. When my efforts don't succeed or the condition continually reappears, I feel victimized."

"Yes, when she uses her vulnerability, weakness, dependency as a weapon to get her way."

"When she gets me excited about some planned activity together and then changes her mind about doing it at the last minute."

"When we date for a while and she tells me she really likes me but isn't ready for a sexual relationship yet, and then she goes and jumps into bed with some guy she meets for the first time."

I think most men have felt victimized at one time or another, as have most women. What's important to look at is how often this occurs.

If I am constantly feeling victimized, there's a good chance I am choosing to play the role of a victim. I know a woman who is always being victimized by men, but she is also always being victimized by her employers, her car, life in general. She is choosing to play the role of a victim, because it brings her some kind of rewards—maybe sympathy, maybe avoiding the success she's afraid of in these areas. A vital point I make in my workshops is that we are all neurotic to some extent; we'll never get rid of all our unhealthy fears, beliefs, games.

The key to success in life is not becoming perfect emotionally, but learning to deal with the obstacles that stand between us and what we really want. If feeling victimized once in a while doesn't get in the way of having healthy and satisfying relationships, then it's no problem.

The Liberated Man Meets the Liberated Woman

Even as they are growing and changing, one thing that threatens men most, confuses them most, frightens them most, is the persona of the newly liberated, independent, strong-minded woman who wants what she wants and knows how to ask for it.

As we discuss some of the specific instances of male responses to the changing role of women, I'd like to make *my* position clear. My only complaint about the women's movement is that it downgrades women in trying to establish their equality to men. I always thought women were superior. I honestly believe that women are just as intelligent, more creatively intuitive, more compassionate, more sexual, more sensual, more able to cope with change, more spontaneous, and more fun than most men. And most of the men interviewed for this book agree. We've already heard them say women are better at being in touch with and expressing their feelings. (See the answers to Question 68 earlier in this chapter.) How about the other areas of male-female interaction?

82. Do you think women are superior to men in any other ways?

"Intuition."

"I believe God made them the stronger sex because they produce all the babies."

"Relationships."

"Yes. That is, they have their admirable qualities that help to support a man in a complete relationship."

"Yes, the ability to deal with stress . . . and they live longer."

"In general, they are more willing to grow and change."

"Women excel at yielding and surrendering. They are more intuitive, more holistic."

                        *   *   *

These men are liberated from many of the traditional
male stereotypes and role models, and they admire
women in many ways. But they can still be scared off by
them.

Do these men really want their women to be liberated?

83. Do you really want a woman to be liberated and independent . . . or do you go along with this because it pleases them and gets you more of what you want?

*"Prefer her to be liberated. Then she's not working out of
dependence, and I don't feel like she's expecting me to 'take care
of her.' "*

*"Liberated and independent women are more exciting, less
boring, able to teach me about life, as opposed to solely the reverse.
More sharing occurs."*

*"I like a woman to be in control of her own life—therefore she
is in or out of my life under her own power."*

*"I get much more satisfaction in attracting a strong, indepen-
dent woman than a needy, unhappy-without-a-man type."*

"I really like a liberated woman."

*"Obviously there's a selfish aspect to all of it, but I think that
basically I want what's best for people's highest good, because it's
better to be around happy, fulfilled people than sad ones. . . . Plus,
I believe in wishing unto others what I wish for myself."*

*"I really want my sister humans to be liberated and indepen-
dent, but I feel somehow we are all losing something culturally by
making the sexes more equal, more similar."*

I suppose this was sort of a loaded question, but the men
gave answers that were indicative of their own security
and self-confidence and of their willingness to relate to
women as people. Our higher selves definitely outscored
our lower ones on this question.

84. Do you think the women's movement has made women more feminine and desirable, or less?

Only eight men out of 101 thought that the "new woman" was less desirable and feminine. The most interesting of the negative responses—*"More conscious, but less desirable. Somehow it screws up the male-female energy."*—came from the forty-nine-year-old minister and family therapist who's been married three times. This remark reflects fears men have that some of the cultural, emotional, material benefits of the traditional male-female relationship have been lost in the move toward total sexual parity. I feel that this doesn't have to be the case, and the women I know and respect most in the women's movement are not trying to eliminate warmth, nurturing, supportiveness, and sensitivity. Most of the men interviewed are in agreement on this and feel that liberated women are much more desirable and feminine.

"I think the pendulum is swinging back. Initially less, and now it's becoming more."

"More! They think for themselves as opposed to being submissive. Independent women are more exciting and desirable to me!"

"More feminine and desirable . . . and certainly more available."

"I think a stronger woman has stronger sexual attraction for me."

"Much much more. In comparison, the nonliberated woman is like a cardboard cutout—no life, no vitality!"

"They're more frightening; I'm less sure of myself. But no doubt about it, they are sexier and more fun to be with."

"I find a liberated woman much more willing to give me what I want, as if she's trying to prove she's still feminine and desirable . . . and she is!"

85. What do you think is the biggest gain for men from the women's movement?

"*Women are more assertive sexually, and they like men who aren't macho.*"

"*We've gotten just as liberated as they have from the old roles.*"

"*Liberated sex.*"

"*Women telling us what they want.*"

"*Stark terror. And those who survive that get a lot of personal growth and self-discovery.*"

"*Freedom from traditional male roles.*"

"*It's produced much more interesting women.*"

"*Women's self-confidence.*"

"*It has taken a lot of the burden off us men, in that we no longer have to totally support them, constantly bolster their fragile egos, and put up with their frustrations at not being able to fend for themselves.*"

"*Women are more assertive in all areas.*"

And here's the obvious follow-up question:

86. What is your biggest complaint about the women's movement?

"*Just as chauvinistic as the system they're trying to change.*"

"*Vitriolic ladies who condemn us for chauvinistic words when it would be better to gently teach and inform us.*"

"*It has turned some women into fanatics.*"

"*Sometimes too extreme.*"

"*Women who are hypersensitive about words, [who have] a tendency to attack or blame men.*"

"*They seem to want equality in everything but responsibility.*"

"*The double binds between what women say they want and oftentimes what their actions show they really want.*"

"*Women can forget that there are some very positive differences between them and men.*"

"*Belligerency and anger.*"

"*That part of it is still angry* (MS. *magazine, for example*). *Love works!*"

"Self-sufficient women who think they can manage without men."

It's important to realize that these complaints come from a special group of men who generally applaud the gains women have made over the past two decades. Of course, as women get more of what they want, they are more willing to be feminine and desirable, more willing to treat men as fellow human beings rather than adversaries. I've never been very threatened by the women's movement, having always enjoyed the company of strong and independent women.

My first experience with a spokeswoman for the movement itself happened in 1970, when I interviewed Kate Millett for NBC Radio in New York. She had just published *Sexual Politics,* and I must admit that I was expecting a fire-breathing dragon to arrive. Instead, this energetic bundle of nervous energy showed up in sweatshirt and jeans, carrying a granny dress on a hanger—she wasn't sure whether this was to be a radio or TV show. We introduced ourselves, and she asked if it was O.K. for her to park in front of the station in Rockefeller Plaza. I told her it was definitely a towaway zone, so she begged me to come downstairs and help her find a place to park. I did so. When we returned to the studio, she said she simply couldn't go on without coffee, so I ran up to the commissary and got her a cup. At this point I felt more as if I had been running errands for Scarlett O'Hara than visiting with one of the most feared members of the women's movement. Throughout the interview, she was charming, feminine, and very outspoken. She was not afraid to demand what she thought women deserved, nor was she afraid to let her womanly nature express itself.

I think what turned a lot of men off to the women's

movement was the fact that they only heard the strident words, without being exposed to the soft and gentle women behind the words.

One situation that comes up more often with a liberated woman than with a more traditional woman is the issue of who pays for what in a relationship. In the traditional male-female roles, the man pays for everything, the assumption being that he is the earner, while her main role is to bring him support, pleasure, and whatever he needs to keep him happy and willing to pay the bills. Women quite understandably rebelled against this, saying it smacked of a form of prostitution, the man buying the woman's favors and affection.

I caused quite a stir in the early 1970s when I addressed a National Organization of Women chapter and pointed out that men had been paying the check in restaurants for years, but women thought it somehow created equity if they now offered to pay their fair share, . . . rarely going beyond that to pay the entire check even when they could well afford it. After my talk, three women came up and invited me out to dinner!

This is still an uncomfortable issue for a lot of men, and many women tell me they've had major hassles with men unwilling to let them pay their own way. They see it as the man's wanting to hold on to control of the situation. I see it more as some men wanting to keep things the way they were because this is more comfortable for them. Frankly, I admire women who have liberated themselves in this situation. If I had been culturally trained to let women pay the entire bill when we went out, I'm not sure I'd be willing to let go of that expectation.

87. Do you prefer that a woman you are going out with automatically offer to pay her share of the

restaurant check, or do you prefer she assume you will pay . . . or would you rather not discuss this? More than half the men responding said their strong preference is that the woman offer to pay her share, with occasional treats by both the man and the woman. About 20 percent of the men, mostly those in their forties, fifties, and sixties, said they prefer that the woman assume the man will pay. (Most of these men are also in quite high-income brackets.) The rest said either they wanted to discuss it or it depended on the relative income levels of the two people involved. A few of the answers:

"Usually I pay, though I had one great experience in a four-star restaurant when a woman surreptitiously paid. It was a wonderful high!"

"If I make more, I should usually pay. If she makes more, she should pay more often."

"I'd rather she offer to pay her share, and discuss this before the check arrives. Otherwise, to switch off, with each of us treating at different times. That's the most fun once a dating pattern has been established."

"I enjoy it either way. It really depends on the relationship and what is fair."

"I'm lucky to be going with a successful and generous woman who loves to pick up the check. At first I felt a bit funny about this, but she makes twice as much money as me, so why not? And I do treat her once in a while, too, and buy her nice little gifts. I think we have a very loving arrangement, and it's one of the things that makes her irresistible to me. I've dated many other women who see themselves as liberated and earn good money but still refuse to even go 'dutch.' I think a lot of men don't bring it up because they've met women who would just say no, and that's damned embarrassing."

"I love treating a woman to dinner, but not if it becomes the norm, something she takes for granted. So I really hang out only

with women who pay their own way, and when I treat them, it's a real treat, not something I'm doing because they expect it."

"My partner has told me that she doesn't feel comfortable paying her own way, so I gave in on this, but it irks me from time to time. We earn about the same amount of money, and she's salting a lot more away in the bank than I am—a lot of it that she's saved because she didn't pay her half of a lot of dinner checks. I have this vision of us splitting someday and her taking that money out of the bank and giving it to some man who's more assertive about this than I am."

This is still a touchy subject for men and women. Since 1978, when my book *Moneylove* came out, I've been conducting prosperity consciousness workshops around the world, teaching people to look at their basic emotional attitudes toward money and success and to see their money as an extension of the love they are willing to give and receive. When couples get caught up in the petty details of who's going to pay a $15 or $20 check, it's very hard for them to allow real prosperity into their lives. This issue has to be clarified as soon as possible in a relationship, without rancor and with all of the feelings it kicks off being openly expressed.

I once lived with a woman who had some real insecurities about money. She had been used to having financial things taken care of, first by her parents, then by her husband of thirteen years. Though she had a healthy income when I met her, she told me that she absolutely couldn't handle paying her own way in a restaurant. I had two choices: to end the relationship or to see whether we could come up with some form of compromise. (Of course, I could also have tried to change her mind, but after some initial efforts at this I realized it was only creating distance between us.) What we worked out was a simple and fair exchange. I paid for the food, both when eating out and at home. She did all the cooking and washed the dishes. By working this out, we removed an element of conflict from our relationship: between my belief that there should be financial sharing between couples and her finding it very difficult to pay her own way. I should report that this created an atmosphere in which she could choose to change on her own. We haven't been together for several years but are still good friends. She pays her own way in her current relationship and offers to do so when the two of us meet for lunch. It doesn't matter how it's worked out, as long as it's done ahead of time, so that the issue doesn't get ignited every time we end up in a restaurant.

Most of the men, myself included, prefer that it's automatically assumed each person will pay his or her share of the check. That way it doesn't create any conflict; it's more fun than occasionally picking up the entire check as a special treat.

All these suggestions have to be taken with a large dose of common sense. If the woman earns $15,000 or less per year, while the man earns $200,000, his offering to pay the complete bill will enable them to eat out more often and in better restaurants. But even in situations like this, it's usually healthier for the relationship if the woman at least offers to pay her own way, so that they can set the ground rules at the beginning.

Since I've conducted hundreds of workshops on dealing with money in our lives, I've learned how emotionally repressed we all are in this area. Most people would rather tell you the intimate details of their sexual lives than reveal how much money they earn or have. What seems to hurt many relationships is that the money issues are discussed much too late, usually after the couple has started living together or gotten married. Since I am most interested in a relationship with a woman who can take care of herself financially, I make it a point to find this out very quickly. And I have been with women who are in much better financial shape than I am. It feels wonderful, and I can't really understand men who have trouble with this. The men in this survey don't have any such trouble at all.

88. Do you feel comfortable being with a woman who earns as much as or more than you?

Only two men said they prefer being with women who earn less than they do. Most of the rest just answered "yes," with an occasional comment.

"And how! My dream is to be kept."
"My wife brought a half-million-dollar inheritance into our relationship, and it's freed us from the everyday hassles that can get in the way of love."
"I like it when she's very successful, but I might feel uncomfortable if she earned more doing the same work I do."

Most of the men said they prefer that expenses be shared equally in a relationship and that money be pooled in a marriage or deeply committed living-together relationship. However, a majority felt that what each person had before the relationship started should remain his or her own.

89. If you had to choose, wouldn't you really rather have a woman who was gorgeous, sexy, and a wonderful cook than one who had made her mark in an exciting career?

Trick questions didn't work very well with this group. Most of the men said they wanted all four and saw no reason why they should have to make a choice. A large number of the men responding *already have* all four. My point in asking the question was to see if, despite their commitment to liberation for women, these men had, at some deep-down level, a desire for an old-fashioned woman who stayed at home and only worked at keeping them happy. Perhaps I should have asked that question directly, but I'm sure the answer would have been the same, since most of the men are already getting it all.

"Really . . . I'll take gorgeous, sexy, and 'has made her mark in an exciting career' . . . preferably a restaurant critic."

"I insist on all four. Actually, outward qualities like the ones you describe are not good indicators of the intelligence, independence, and exciting presence that I look for in a woman."

"I'd like it all, but the career woman is very attractive."

"Gorgeous, sexy . . . and since we're both in exciting and profitable careers, we hired a cook!"

"No, I want it all, and I've got it."

"I'm gorgeous, sexy, a great cook, and in an exciting career. Why should I settle for less in a woman?"

"Hard to say. If she's gorgeous and sexy and has made her mark, we can go out to eat at will . . . but I really enjoy cooking, myself."

The one dissenting vote—*"Yes. You can't go to bed with an exciting career, especially if she's ugly."*—came from a forty-nine-year-old investor with a degree in economics. He was divorced in 1976 after fourteen years of marriage and has recently ended a five-year living-together relationship. He says he does not want a major relationship at this time, just casual companionship and romance. I mention this because it's interesting that he's the only man who answered the question this way, and also one of the few who isn't either in a relationship now or totally open to having one.

90. **How important is it that a woman you are attracted to have her own career, one you can respect?**

"Very important."

"It helps."

"Very. I like independent women."

"Very important. Really vital."

"It is important, but only because I want my woman to be self-actualizing, lively, full of energy and interest, and not dependent on me for these things. I want a peer, not a dependent."

I did not expect such vehemence on this question. These men really *want* women to have exciting and interesting careers. The largest group of answers were simply "Very," "Important," and "Very important." These three answers accounted for almost half the responses. The others were either elaborations on the same answer or, in a few cases, more moderately stated—it was fairly important or somewhat important. Only *two* men actually said it wasn't at all important to them. And one of these hedged his bet by saying, *"Not at all, but if she has a demeaning career, I'm not very tolerant."*

Since a lot of women are concerned that men may resent their careers or be jealous of them, this is important and valuable for them to hear. It will also help men who wonder if being with a woman in a successful career is worthwhile.

I also asked the question of the members of the men's discussion group I attended.

Pat: *"I won't accept anything less than a woman who is as involved in her life as I am in mine. And it's got to be somebody who's got some kind of a career, not a homemaker, housewife, dishwasher, floor scrubber. That's boring. If I want a maid, I can go hire one. I don't want that in a female companion-lover."*

Joe: *"I definitely want a woman who has a career that's important to her, although it could just as easily be strong interests she's involved in instead of a career. But she has to be involved in something of her own."*

Steve: *"Well, I've been in some relationships where the woman was so involved in her career she just didn't have much time to get together. So it's real important that they make enough time to put the relationship on a high priority."*

Jay: *"It's real important for me to have a woman whose work I can respect, who's real involved in her work—otherwise she's going to be making a lot of demands on me. Because I want to spend a lot of time on my work. But I don't want somebody who is so preoccupied with her work that she doesn't have energy for the relationship or the traditional woman's roles. I prefer to do more of the traditional male things, and I prefer a woman who's more into the female roles. I like to cook, and it would be neat to have a woman who could tune up my car, but I prefer that most of the time she cook and let me tune up the car. I like a woman who's into making a home, but not so that's her whole life. I like a woman who's perhaps more oriented in that direction than I am, maybe less career-oriented than I am. I want her to enjoy homemaking as part of her life, but definitely not as the main thing that she does."*

Josh: *"I agree it's important that she not be so into her career that she doesn't have enough time for me, but I really enjoy the sharing of events and ideas concerning our respective work. I want a woman in some kind of creative career, something that stimulates and excites her, so that she can excite me with her alive feelings about it. Though I don't demand it, I would also like a woman to enjoy cooking for me and cleaning up the house, though I guess we could hire people to do that. I just love lying in bed at night and discussing what went on for us during the day. I would be bored stiff if the only things that went on for her were cooking, cleaning, and shopping."*

*   *   *

I wondered whether these men had any preferences in
the kinds of careers or professions they wanted the women
in their lives to have:

91. What careers do you find most interesting and attractive for a woman to have?

"Any career that makes her an interesting and attractive person."

"The most interesting women in my life have been psychologists or involved in growth in some way or another."

"Preferably someone offering a service I could enjoy, like a masseuse or gourmet cooking teacher."

"Professional women—lawyers, doctors, business administrators, etc.—are the most intriguing, perhaps because they fit the traditional mode the least."

"Entrepreneurial or creative."

"Artists, dancers, designers, musicians."

"Medical profession, corporate executive."

"Something glamorous, like a dancer, artist, actress, magazine editor . . . or something unusual, like a pilot, brain surgeon, professional athlete. I also seem very attracted to women who own their own businesses."

"For some reason, college professors turn me on, especially since I never went to college."

"Therapists, masseuses and other body workers, creative artists of any kind."

"As a writer, it's great to find another writer or an editor. Actually, if I could have my ideal fantasy, it would be to meet a beautiful woman who owns her own successful publishing house!"

Slightly more than half the men responding had no
specific preference at all. They just wanted women to be
in careers that interested and fulfilled *them.*

92. **Do you have any difficulty giving a woman the time and space to have her own life, her own friends outside the relationship?**

"As long as it doesn't interfere with our relationship."

"Only if she sees the same male friend more than once a week."

"I have some difficulty, but I value her independence."

"No, I want a woman to have that. In fact, I consider it an essential part of the relationship, so the woman can grow and bring that growth back to the relationship."

"Sometimes, if she doesn't seem to be available for me. Part of the reason . . . maybe the main reason I get into a committed relationship is because we both want to spend more time together. If her outside interests get in the way of this, I would seriously consider downgrading my commitment."

Most of the men said they had no difficulty whatsoever here; about one fourth added that this was so as long as it didn't take away from intimate time together. The liberated man enjoys a woman's outside interests, but he doesn't want to feel deprived. In a real sharing relationship, each person will be clear about what he or she wants and needs from the other in terms of time.

93. **Do you really want a woman to have opinions of her own when meeting your friends or business associates, or would you rather she support and agree with you?**

If I had known the results of some of the preceding questions, I probably wouldn't have bothered asking this one, as the answers are predictable.

Most men stressed that they wanted a woman who can think and act for herself and that they found submissive women boring. A few added that it is nice when the woman has her own opinions and these happen to support or coincide with their own.

In going back and checking this out with a few of the men, I asked whether they weren't really more likely to be attracted to or involved with women who had similar values, who would be unlikely to have opinions strongly opposing theirs. The response to this was also predictable. Without exception, they said they want women to have and express their own opinions, but they strongly prefer that these opinions be compatible with their own.

As one man put it: *"I'd have to be something of a masochist to choose a woman with very conflicting views to mine on major issues. Then we'd be spending a lot of our time competing or arguing rather than sharing and cooperating."*

Responses to the next question were similar.

94. If a woman has some interests you don't share, do you feel O.K. if she pursues them on her own?

I won't even bother to record the answers here, as most of them were simple declarations such as "Absolutely," "Sure," "Of course," "Certainly."

Though this question is related to Question 92, it is more specific in some ways. In the past, men and women were more likely to give up outside interests not shared by their partner, so as to avoid jealousy or confrontation. I know one couple that got a divorce primarily because he couldn't handle the fact that she liked to go hiking and mountain climbing without him. Jealousy was involved here, because she usually found it easy to locate other men interested in these activities, usually in groups. The multiple threat of her doing something she loved to do without him, something she was much better at than he, and something she often did with other men was just too much.

As couples become more liberated from old habits and roles, they begin to understand the importance of each person having separate interests. They recognize it as a way of keeping the relationship from stagnating. Any creative effort will stagnate in the absence of new blood and new ideas being brought in once in a while.

95. Do you see women as having any privileges or advantages over men today that you would like to have?

Ninety-three percent of the men saw no such privileges or advantages they also wanted for themselves. Only a couple of interesting answers came from the few who did see this.

"I think they still get away with being "taken care of" more than we do."

"They use their sexuality more openly than we men could ever get away with."

Several of the men said they thought women started out as more aware and more caring in a relationship, but felt that they themselves had acquired these traits, too, so women no longer had this advantage.

The men interviewed in this survey still have some fears concerning women and relationships, but much less than reported among the general male population. They seem content with their current male role and the independent women they encounter. They have diminished whatever fear they originally had by taking action, by plunging ahead into relationships with strong women and quickly learning the advantages of doing so. Most of the men, instead of saying and feeling "I am afraid of this," can more accurately declare, "I used to be afraid of this." And almost all of the men would agree that no matter how threatening or scary women sometimes are, the idea of being alone and without love is much more so.

4

KEEPING
IN TOUCH

96. Are you now getting enough affection in your life?

"Plenty of sex, but not really enough affection. That's why I am ready for a strong relationship with a woman."

"Yes, better than ever, thanks to a loving wife and lots of good friends."

"Not quite."

"I get enough affection; what I often miss is romance."

"Most of the time."

"I want more."

"No, I could always use more."

"I come from a big loving family, lots of hugs and kisses, and I miss that now, even though I live with a wonderful woman . . . she can't give me all the affection I think I need."

*   *   *

About half the men answered "yes" to this question. Many of those who express a desire for more affection also describe themselves as being in very satisfying love relationships. What this indicates is that many men, in or out of a relationship feel the deprivation that most of us suffer, the deprivation of enough nonsexual touching.

From the moment of birth, every human being desperately needs the loving touch of other human beings in order to survive and grow emotionally and physiologically. Scientists have discovered that babies who are not touched enough can develop all sorts of medical problems, and there is every indication that we never outgrow this basic human need. It cannot be fulfilled by sexual activity alone.

Most of the men interviewed for this book are touchers. It's amazing that more men aren't, considering how much more attracted loving women are to men who are good at hugging, stroking, and massaging . . . not to mention the fact that touchers are much happier much more of the time than nontouchers. It is, however, difficult for many men to reach out in nonsexual ways to women . . . and impossible for some to reach out to other men, unless it's during some body contact sport "approved" by the male community.

I remember a good male friend who hadn't seen me in some months grabbing me in a warm, loving hug and kissing my cheek. This was about twelve years ago. I think all the blood must have rushed out of my face, because he looked at me with concern and asked if I was all right. I had never hugged a man before in my life and was just feeling the natural shock of experiencing something unknown and frightening. But then I decided I enjoyed his affectionate greeting, and we always introduced ourselves that way from then on. I must confess that knowing he was heterosexual helped make it O.K. at the time. I've since hugged hundreds of men of all sexual persuasions, and it's felt wonderful.

The women I've talked to have all said they are more open to men who can touch other men in affectionate ways. But women have been taught that it's O.K. to touch a member of the same sex; we men haven't. We still have some powerful conditioning to overcome in order to free ourselves in this area. Since becoming comfortable hugging a man, I find I am much better at touching women —more sensitive, a better lover.

In 1975, I conducted a workshop on "The Intimate Touch," advertised in a brochure as exploring the sensual versus the sexual capabilities of men and women. I was hoping for an equal distribution of the sexes, so that we could do a lot of pairing up for the touching and massaging exercises I had planned for the two-hour session. Thirty-two men and two women showed up! At first I panicked; I seriously considered cancelling the workshop and sending everyone home. Luckily, I realized how very narrow-minded of me that would be. I was honest and told the group that I had wanted a more even distribution. But what I wanted to teach them was a very loving hand massage, one both men and women could use with members of the opposite sex as a form of nonsexual touching in a romantic setting. Not one of the people there took up my offer of a full refund, and it was one of the most caring workshops I've ever presented. Several of the men came up to me afterwards and said they had stayed because of how I had described the workshop—as a way to learn skills that would serve them well, providing something very special they could give a woman they cared about. While ordinarily they wouldn't have felt comfortable doing any kind of massage on a man, or receiving from a man, they now realized that they could have missed a very satisfying experience.

Most men I know, myself included, would much prefer a loving massage delivered by a warm and lovely woman. What I have learned in twelve years of growing and expanding my horizons is that there's no need to be deprived when a woman isn't available to give me the touch I want. A good male friend can give me a wonderful massage. I can even do a pretty good job on myself if no one else is available. I don't have to present the woman in my life with all of my touch needs. That can be a tremendous burden to lay at someone's door.

An even bigger burden is to demand that all our touch needs be provided during the sex act. If having sex is the only way we can get physically close to another person, then we are missing something vital in our lives. Our skin is actually our largest single organ, many times larger than our genitals and with a lot more territory to cover. Concentrating on giving and receiving physical pleasure in just one or two small parts of the body leads to desensitization and emotional malnutrition. As men open up and become aware of the joys of nonsexual touching, they get more for themselves in and out of relationships. They are able to give much more. A very accurate slogan might be: "Touchers get more of what they want."

97. What is the most pleasurable physical activity you've had with a woman without sex?

"Having her massage my scalp."

"Sharing a massage."

"Just cuddling and holding each other close for hours and hours."

"Just sleeping with a beautiful and loving woman I was friends with."

"Dancing, skiing, backrubs, snuggling, hugging."

"Slow dancing."

"Cuddling, massage, hugging, touching."

"Sailing and tennis."

148

*   *   *

Several of the men described athletic or outdoor activities, leading me to surmise they haven't yet discovered the pleasures of nonsexual touching.

98. Can you enjoy cuddling with a woman even if she says she's not interested in sex with you?

"Definitely. Touching is wonderful!"

"Yes, particularly if I'm attracted to her . . . there's always hope."

"Definitely. My best friendships have been that way."

"I love cuddling, whether sex is included or not. If I have a choice, I prefer getting to know a woman by cuddling with her before we ever have sex. It's a way to find out if she really is warm and affectionate . . . much more important qualities to me than pure animal passion."

Only three men responded with negative answers to this question. One said he considered all touching foreplay.

Most of the men have learned they can get more of what they want by having alternative ways of getting physical pleasure for themselves. Some years ago, my friend Dr. Leo Buscaglia told me he felt the surest way to achieve success in any field was to have as many alternatives as possible. In recent years, more and more men have been discovering that one of the nicest alternatives is to have good women friends as well as women lovers.

99. Do you have any women friends you enjoy being with but are not interested in sexually?

"Yes, my ex-wife. In fact, we are much better friends than we were spouses. I'll even go over sometimes and spend the night with her, cuddling and talking."

"Oh yes."

"Many! My women friends are extremely important, as they

*are more sensitive than my men friends, and it's wonderful being
with a woman in a nonsexual manner."*

*"Absolutely, and I always have. Friendships are more endur-
ing than love affairs."*

Almost all affirmative answers on this one, but I had left
something out. I went back and asked a number of the
men whether they *actually had* nonsexual touching experiences with their women friends. Most said they enjoyed
cuddling, walking hand in hand with, hugging, and/or
massaging their women friends. A lot of physical nourishment was provided in these friendships, particularly when
one or both friends was not currently in a love relationship.

100. **Would you rather be with a nonsexual but enjoyable woman friend or with an attractive
woman who offers you quick sexual release and
nothing else?**

I asked this question because of my own preference for
being with a friendly cuddling companion rather than
someone just interested in genital contact and orgasm. Of
course, both combined are delightful, but if I have to have
one without the other, I'll take the nonsexual closeness of
a touchable friend.

"This is a stacked question. Of course, the friend."

*"I receive much more from a woman friend. A quick sexual
release is nice but very boring."*

*"The friend, without a doubt. But an occasional quickie has
its place, too."*

Near unanimous agreement, so maybe the question was
stacked in favor of the friend.

We make initial contacts with the opposite sex as teenagers, usually, and quite often the primary desire is for closeness and gentle physical contact. In this age of sexual freedom, however, we tend to equate physical contact with making sexual overtures. The sexual approach becomes a habit, subsequently we go through life missing out on a lot of physical pleasure and emotional satisfaction we could be getting from people outside of sex or romance.

This is one aspect of interpersonal relating in which men have much more conditioning to overcome than women, much more to learn. I was pleasantly surprised, therefore, at the answers to the following question:

101. **What are some unique ways in which women have touched you either sexually or nonsexually that have felt especially good?**

"I love to have a woman's fingers run through my hair."

"My legs. One woman loved to stroke and play with my legs, a part that often gets neglected in touching."

"Bonnie was a lady I never had sex with, but when we were driving she would hold on to my leg in a very cozy, cuddly way that I can't really describe—it felt as if we really belonged together. She just melted next to me in a car."

"Just rubbing me all over with her hands."

"She would pull my hair—grab a hunk of it in her hand and gently tug at it. It felt great, and I've since done it for a lot of women who also really love it."

"She would drive me crazy just playing with my hand—in a movie or even at a restaurant—running her fingers over it, caressing it, sucking on my fingers. I've been with women and had great sexual experiences that hardly matched what she could do just by playing with my hand!"

"My current woman has a way of touching me anywhere with love that just feels completely different from any other touch I've ever had. It's as if she's totally focused on the part she's touching, as if nothing else exists for her at that moment . . . and I've never

felt as completely loved by another human being."

"I love to have her run her fingernails over my arm, my back, my legs . . . anywhere."

"One woman I dated loved to put her arm around my shoulder and just gently hold my earlobe between her fingers. I always remember how that felt, even though it was about six years ago."

The reason for my pleasant surprise was that 90 percent of the touching the men described as feeling especially good was sensual, loving touching, rather than sexual touching. Several of the men said they really liked to have their genitals touched even when not in a sexual mood or with a sex partner. This came up in some preliminary interviews, so I specifically added the following question:

102. **Would you feel good having a woman caress your genitals even though, for whatever reason, she let you know that she didn't want to have sex with you or have you ejaculate?**

"I dated one woman several years ago who was very sweet and had just had a horrible relationship break up. She told me right up front that she wouldn't feel good having sex with me, since she needed time to recover, but she would really like being with me. We ended up one evening at her place, and we gave each other massages. We were lying there nude, in each other's arms, and she asked me if I was feeling sexually frustrated. I told her the truth, that it felt very good, but that I hadn't really thought about having sex with her because she had ruled it out at the beginning, and that if she wanted to change the rules, I'm sure I could change my feelings about this. She said it was still important for her to remain celibate for a while, but she liked the closeness, and if I thought it wouldn't be painful for me, she would like to place her head between my legs and rest her cheek against my crotch. She did and I got hard, but reassured her that I did not have to come to feel good, that it felt good just feeling the warmth of her cheek.

Since I was having an active sexual life with another woman I was dating, it wasn't sexually frustrating to be with this woman, and we often spent the night together, with her falling asleep with her face in my crotch. It sounds silly to tell about it, but there was something very sweet and innocent about it. We never did have sex together, since I went on a three-month trip and she was in love when I came back, but I always remember the feeling of her warm cheek against my penis."

"Yes, as long as my sexual needs were being met, it would feel good."

"I think it's great. It's nice and relaxing and very caring, there's a lovingness about it."

"I'm going now with a woman who may not always be into making love, but always seems to like having her hands between my legs. In other words, she doesn't ignore my genitals when she's not in the mood for sex. My genitals are not off limits when we're in nonsexual spaces."

"If the feeling were mutual, I think it would be fine, though I might wonder about her motives."

Only six men answered "no" to this one, three of them adding that it would be too frustrating. It's heartening to note that most of the men were willing to experience some new alternatives in touching, and the unique feeling of having their genitals stroked in a nonsexual manner. And that a number of them had, in fact, already had this as part of their touching history. Our genitals are not some detached mechanism that only comes alive, that only feels, when sex is happening or about to happen.

In our culture, we have certain gender role stereotypes, certain preconceived notions about what men like and what women like, what men do and what women do. For instance, most people believe, because we've been taught to believe, that women enjoy touching more than men and that men see touch as mainly the means to an end, namely, sex. This is changing, but as with all firmly implanted ideas, it will take some years before there is a complete transformation, before new male and female babies are taught differently in significant numbers to change the prevailing stereotype. In the meantime, each of us can make our own dent in this wall of antiquated beliefs. Men can be more willing to reach out in loving, friendly touch, and to just lie back and enjoy touch in and of itself. Women can be our teachers in this, as in so many things, for they've had more experience and more tactile skills.

103. How do you like to touch a woman in public, and what do you want her response to be?

104. How do you like a woman to touch you in public?

These two questions obviously go together. I wanted to find out if these men are willing to be tender and affectionate in public and, if so, how so.

"(102) I love to hug my woman in public, to tell the world how I feel about her and maybe do a bit of bragging. And I like her to really melt into my arms and get into it. (103) I enjoy having her hold my hand or put her arm around the small of my back."

"Often. Often. Often!"

"(102) Hold hands, pat, touch, stroke, nuzzle, light caress and occasional goose. I want her response to be alert, present, willing, and clear about her limits. (103) All of the above, provided they are expressive of her energy and not attempts to elicit responses from me."

"So much can be conveyed by touch. When her hand is on my arm or her arm is around me, I can tell if she is bored and wants to go home, if she is feeling very loving toward me, or if she is somewhat distant. I want her to be receptive to my every mood and touch. I like to touch her to reassure her that I am still loving her, but I don't want her response to be a demand for more attention.

I feel most of our touching should take place in private. I am always suspicious of those lovey-dovey couples who can't keep their hands off each other in public, and I think that they probably aren't into much affection in private. I don't want her touching me as a signal to the world that she belongs to me—that kind of holding-on-for-protection grip. I guess my favorite way to touch her in public is to have my hand resting on her thigh under the table at a restaurant or in the dark at a movie theater, so maybe that doesn't really count as public. And I like her hand on top of mine or holding mine on her thigh . . . or reaching over to touch my thigh."

"Lovingly all the way around."

"Handholding, hugging. Clandestine moments are good, too. I'd like her to respond naturally. And I want her to touch me the same way."

"Discreet touching, which I like to have reciprocated."

"(102) I'm a toucher and feel comfortable kissing and hugging in public. Mostly, I'd like the response to be mutual. (103) The same, although I find there are situations where my priorities are elsewhere and kissing and hugging just gets in the way."

"Holding hands. Arm in arm, arm around waist."

"Arm in arm. Sneak a pat on the ass when nobody's looking and have it reciprocated."

"There's almost a magnetic pull from a woman when I really care about her, and my hands naturally gravitate to her body. I love to touch her hair, her face, her arms, put my arms around her—anything that feels comfortable for her and me in public. And I like to feel her doing the same—a light, caressing, gentle touch, just letting me know that she's there and cares."

Those men who responded with only one answer indicated that, for them, Question 102 had the same answer as 103. These men do not want blatant sexual touching or lots of kissing in public. Only one man even mentioned kissing as something he wanted to do in public. Several told me that women who always need strong affectionate displays in public really turn them off, that they feel this is not a healthy loving response. Rather, they see it as the sign of someone who needs constantly to be reassured.

If I were to draw a conclusion from the large majority of these responses, I would have to say that sensitive men want women to feel free to touch them, and they want to be free in the same way. They want the touch to be tender and dignified in public. The kind of women these men most easily fall in love with are those who can convey a world of caring through a light and subtle touch.

I've saved one answer for last, because I enjoyed it so much:

"Eileen and I have this secret thing we do in public. Whenever one of us holds or caresses the other's little finger, it means that we are especially turned on right then and would like nothing better than to be able to tear our clothes off and make beautiful, passionate love right then and there. It's very exciting and playful, and I just love it when I touch her little finger and she gives me a knowing, accepting smile that tells me she's in the same place."

Perhaps what we most enjoy having touched is our imaginations.

In my own experience, I've found that sexual activity is not really that different with different partners—nowhere near as different as the nonsexual or presexual touches between two individuals. No two women have ever touched me in exactly the same way, and there are women I've known and loved who could touch me in the dark after ten or fifteen years, and I would know them instantly —the way they rest a hand on the inside of my elbow, press a finger behind my ear, grab a handful of hair, or press their arm against mine, different in all the variations of pressure, actual skin surface covered, and even temperature.

As we become more sensitized to touch, we open up a whole new realm of pleasure possibilities.

5

THE
POST-SEXUAL
REVOLUTION

105. Now that women are more sexually available without marriage, are you more likely to enter a deeply committed relationship?

"The two are unrelated. Sex has always been available."

"Less likely."

"No change either way."

"My fantasies have all been acted out. I am all the more deeply committed to monogamy."

"Now that women are stronger and more willing to be on their own without a main man in their life, a committed relationship somehow seems more special, as if, for the first time, a woman is giving up as much as a man to be in one."

"Less likely, since I now am seeing three warm and passionate

women on a regular basis . . . and I really feel spoiled for a one-to-one commitment."

"More likely to enter into one. Probably less likely to stay in it, at least on a monogamous basis."

"I've been married for twenty-five years, and for the past five my wife and I have had an open marriage. It's been exciting and has deepened our love for each other. I don't know of too many other open relationships that have worked, but we have something very special going for us. I think we were both intrigued by the open sexual activity going on around us and felt we had missed something, both having been virgins when we married. I thank God every day for the wonderful woman I'm married to, and if our outside activities ever got in the way of our love for each other, I think we'd both go back to monogamy."

This last comment is interesting, because it points out the failure of one of the most controversial aspects of the sexual revolution: the open marriage.

Nena O'Neill has been a personal friend of mine for over ten years, as was her late husband, George. After they wrote *Open Marriage* in 1972 and it became a huge best seller, they were very dismayed that many people who hadn't read a single page started to experiment with "open marriages." What most people did not know—because they hadn't read the book—was that open sexuality was a very small part of it. What the O'Neills were primarily talking about was open communication between relationship partners. In past years I was often amused and occasionally distressed to find supposedly knowledgeable people telling me that George and Nena (often described just as "those people who wrote *Open Marriage*") were divorced or separated or about to be one or the other. Even talk show hosts and major newspapers and magazines seemed to relish repeating this falsehood. Until George's death two years ago, you couldn't have found a more together couple. I think fears about open relationships motivated a lot of the spreading of this unfounded rumor, as if to say, "Obviously this can't work; it didn't even work for the two people who started it all." Well, they didn't start it all, and what they had—a beautiful loving-together and working-together relationship—worked until death did them part.

Nena O'Neill has told me that through the years she has encountered only a handful of successful open relationships. This happy medium between total unattachment and committed monogamy was probably introduced ahead of its time, as such an arrangement takes much more trust and self-confidence and love than most people bring to relationships.

Other aspects of the sexual revolution have worked out better for all concerned, but men and women still seem confused, as indicated by the responses to the last question. The men fell almost equally into three groups: (1) those who felt themselves less likely to commit to another person, (2) those more likely, and (3) those who didn't see any change at all.

It's also an issue of cause and effect. Are men less likely to make a commitment when they don't have to in order to get their sexual needs met? Or are they now avoiding being seduced into potentially unhealthy relationships and therefore being more selective? Have fewer people been willing at a young age to choose someone to spend the rest of their lives with because of more sexual freedom, or is more sexual freedom simply the result of fewer people marrying at a young age? These issues can be debated back and forth—and will be for many years to come.

In terms of this book, what seemed important to me was to find out specifically what men, each with at least one woman's seal of approval, wanted from women in sexual relationships. And remember, this particular group of men are very much into having committed relationships—76 percent of them have chosen to do so, and most of the rest are available to do so.

106. What are some of the physical things a woman can do to turn you on before first having sex?

More and more women are becoming sexually available; more and more men are learning the pleasures of mutual arousal and mutual sexual relating. Instead of the antiquated man-chases-woman-until-she-lets-him-catch-her scenario, it is becoming commonplace for men to require specific signals from women before initiating sexual activity. A lot of these signals can be physical displays of erotic affection, often simultaneously reciprocated by the man, or almost so.

"Kiss passionately. Touch me erotically. Take my clothes off. Dance nude. Talk erotically. Tease me sexually."

"Her own arousal and the delicacy with which she controls it creates the dance of excitement for me."

"There's a certain change in the feel of her hand on me that lets me know she is aroused and wants to proceed to lovemaking —a certain kind of sexual energy."

"Look me in the eyes and touch me all over!"

"Kissing is nice. Stroking face, arms, legs, and genitals (in that order) is fine. I also love to have my back rubbed."

"Kiss and stroke my body and tell me how beautiful I am."

"Curl up close to me and tell me she is getting excited."

"If she's in the right frame of mind, almost anything she does is a turn-on."

"I have a strong sex drive. Simply being with a 'right' woman is enough of a stimulus."

"Nibble, kiss, and suck my fingers. That always get me going and tells me she is an exciting and responsive lover."

Though most of the men said that very sexually aggressive women could turn them off or make them uncomfortable, once in a while we can respond to a woman who is blatant and aggressive, who has a keen sense of timing and knows when we're ready for such spontaneous behavior. For the most part, there doesn't seem to be any specific thing that women do to turn men on before their first sexual encounter. It's more in the way they do it, in how they project their own arousal to the man.

107. **Do you really prefer a woman to be sexually responsive and open, or do you feel this has taken some of the initiative away from you . . . taken some of the romance and excitement away?**

"I like sexually responsive and open women. This adds to the romance and excitement."

"I don't like acting or contrivance in any form."

"Open and responsive—great! But not to the point of pursuing me, if she wants me . . . she's got to be a bit more clever and coy."

"I think I like women who are comfortable with their own sexuality. On the other hand, I've been avoiding seeing a woman who's been calling me and being very sexually open on the phone. I don't find it a turn-on when I don't know if I even want to be with her. Sexually open and responsive, but only if we have some nice buildup of mutual attraction, and the time to create some kind of connection."

"Open, with gentle assertiveness."

"I really prefer a woman to be sexually responsive and open. I like it when the woman takes the initiative."

"Yes, there is still romance and excitement even when she is open."

Unanimous agreement here. These men want open and responsive women. But most of them also want the woman to be gentle and sensitive to their needs. This doesn't seem to be an unreasonable demand, particularly since women are so much better than men at sensing when the man is ready for lovemaking.

108. How do you want a woman to let you know she's in the mood for lovemaking?

"Genuinely, for her."

"Tell me."

"Touching, fondling, and whispering she's ready."

"By making appropriate comments, facial expression, body language."

"Verbally, if she isn't sure I know."

"Either verbally or by a sign."

"Feminine flirtatiousness is always erotic."

"I don't. I want it to arise between us appropriate to what we are doing."

"Any way is fine, unless she is too aggressive. She can say what she feels (not as a demand though) or touch me."

Only one man out of all those interviewed said he wasn't interested in having the woman let him know when she was in the mood.

In my youth, I always wanted the sexual relationship to happen naturally and spontaneously, without either of us having to say a word. Well, sometimes that happens, but sometimes it doesn't. I think one of the most unfair demands to place on another person in a relationship is that he or she read our mind. There's a belief most people have that "if you loved me, you'd know what I'm thinking." But some people know what I'm thinking and feeling and don't love me, and others love me and haven't the slightest idea what I'm thinking or feeling.

The men responding to this survey want to be told. They want the woman to let them know, directly or indirectly, that she's in the mood. They don't want to play some kind of erotic guessing game.

I mentioned earlier that I think women more readily sense when the man is ready for lovemaking. In discussing this with several sexually aware women, I learned that they usually know when a man is ready for lovemaking. They don't require specific signals from him. So, in this area at least, there is a big difference between what men and women want and need.

109. **Is it important to you that the woman be very skillful and experienced sexually, or do you feel that loving each other will naturally lead to good sex between you?**
"Experience is preferable."

"The more sexually experienced, the better; but I enjoy teaching someone as well."

"Skill is definitely important; freedom from inhibition is more so."

"Experience sure helps!"

"Loving each other leads to good sex if that is what both sincerely want."

"Skill can be natural or learned. Love does not necessarily lead to good sex."

"Yes, there is a strong need for skill and experience, which do not necessarily come from loving each other."

"The skills will develop if the openness is there."

"Skillful is nice. Loving each other doesn't seem to have a lot to do with good sex."

The consensus here is not what I expected it to be. Only eight men out of 101 thought that love automatically produces a good sexual relationship. I'm convinced that a loving, considerate feeling for each other dramatically enhances the sexual experience. Then, in addition, a woman who has learned how to please herself and the man she is with usually makes a more satisfactory sexual partner—

you don't have to concern yourself with the mechanics; you can just relax and enjoy the sharing. Just as I don't want to fly to Europe with a student pilot or have a pre-med student perform surgery on my brain, I prefer that any hit-and-miss sexual learning take place before I enter the picture.

I had the good fortune to have my first sexual relationship with a woman who had been married and divorced. I was inexperienced enough sexually for both of us; her knowledge and loving nature nevertheless made our initial intimate experiences comfortable and satisfying.

I expected that the men surveyed would enjoy the ego gratification of teaching an inexperienced woman. Then again, sometimes it seems that men would like a wonderful sexual partner who knows all the tricks but who has had hardly any actual sexual experience. This survey indicates that love *and* experience are the best recipe for a happy sexual relationship. While not turned on by promiscuity or very aggressive sexual overtures, neither are these men the slightest bit interested in attracting virgins. This is great news for women who often fear that men will be repulsed if they have any sexual history at all. It is a triumph of reality and life experience over myth and old belief systems.

110. **If you knew a woman would get great pleasure in doing anything you wanted her to do for you sexually, what would you have her do . . . in what order?**

Here it is, a chance for the men responding to ask for exactly what they want from a woman sexually.

"Cook dinner (candlelight and wine), cuddle, shower together, massage, make love.

"A slow sensual dance and strip, with her then stripping me, sensually caressing me, and mounting me."

"Massage all over, kiss all over, french-kiss, blow in ear, fellatio, then make mad, passionate love."

"Kissing and hugging. Kissing all over. Stroking body, tummy, legs, and genitals. More kissing, stroking, hugging, squeezing, strong response to my stroking, moans, heavy breathing . . ."

"Dance with me very delicately, swaying without moving our feet. Massage me with oils. Enjoy each other—fingertips, lips, and tongue. Lie very still in tantric entry; devour each other."

"I would start off with a nice relaxing dinner, followed afterward by a soothing backrub and massage—the massage would be done with oil over all of my body. This would last for at least half an hour. Next, she would turn me on my back and initiate oral sex, stopping and starting to get me truly excited. Next, we would make love on a waterbed, in the missionary position—a traditional scenario, but one that would be most pleasurable."

"A great meal with music, candlelight, wine; a bubble bath with fragrant oils; then subtle lights, music, and immersion in erotic love."

These obviously are not men from the old wham-bam-thank-you-ma'am school. As men and women get more sensitized, they see the joys of sexual interaction as being part of a total sensual process. At least half the men wanted massage with oils as a part of their ideal sexual fantasy. Ninety percent of those responding included fellatio as an integral part of their scenario. Since so many men responded in this way, I felt the next six questions would provide more specific information on what they want in oral attention from a woman.

111. How important is it to you that a woman enjoy fellatio?

"Depends on what else she does. I do enjoy it, and haven't been without it enough to say it's not important."

"Well, for me it's been a prerequisite for twenty-five years. I mean, it's just basic . . . and important that the woman is enjoying it and not doing it as an obligation. I always can tell whether it's like a mechanical act or she's really communicating with a sensitive part of me."

"I enjoy oral sex, both the giving and receiving, and the important thing is that the woman does get pleasure out of it."

"On a scale of one to ten, about seven."

"Very important. That's a part of me that's very sensitive."

"Sex is play, whatever we do must be enjoyed by both parties or why do it? I greatly enjoy that kind of play!"

"It's important for my pleasure that a woman does like to orally arouse me, and it's important for me to feel she's enjoying it. . . . I can tell when she's not and nothing turns me off quicker than someone doing something for me because they should or because they want to please me at their own expense!"

"I really think fellatio is much more intimate than intercourse, because she is overcoming a lot of early beliefs that it's dirty or perverted; and because I am being very trusting that she's not going to hurt me, I can't think of any time I'm more vulnerable. So it brings a real closeness to the relationship, but only if she honestly is enjoying the feeling."

"I love fellatio and in my early dating years I'm sure some women did it just as a way of turning me on, without deriving any pleasure from it, and other women so they wouldn't have to have intercourse with me. But as I began being more selective in my sexual partners, and as women began being more honest about their sexual feelings, I've found myself attracting women who just love oral sex. . . . My current lover gets so excited and so into it that if I ever want to have intercourse with her, which we both love as well, I have to stop her and put it inside her. I think I'm the luckiest man in the world to have a woman so turned on to oral sex."

Another unanimous vote. I've always been fascinated by some of the research studies of the fifties and sixties that showed that college-educated men and women were enjoying oral sex much more than those with less education, indicating perhaps that the more educated we were, the less we held on to certain taboos. With a more informed and experienced general population now, I doubt there would be much disputing of the fact that oral sex is a part of most people's sexual pleasure. The more sexually educated and aware men become, the less willing they are to consider intercourse as the be-all and end-all of sexual relations. What has perhaps changed most dramatically is the male concern with female pleasure. There was a time, not too many years ago, when the only question men asked about any sex act performed by or with a woman was, "Does she do it?" The women's movement certainly has succeeded in awakening us men to the necessity of asking, "Does she enjoy it?" And as we become emotionally as well as physically present during sexual relations, we are less willing to be with an unwilling participant, or with someone only doing something for our pleasure rather than her own. In discussions on this subject with men and women, I am becoming more and more convinced that the real sexual revolution is now occurring, and that what it is all about is *both* persons having a wonderful time making love. This synergistic lovemaking, in which the total effect is much greater than just adding two individual erotic experiences, is what most of these men are looking for, and what most of them say they are getting.

112. **Do you enjoy fellatio primarily as a prelude to intercourse, or by itself?**

"A prelude."

"Both, by all means."

"I object to the whole foreplay, intercourse, orgasm sequence as artificial. It is all play whatever happens. Yes, I love it!"

"Either way."

"By itself."

113. Is it important to your pleasure that you ejaculate in her mouth?

"No, and I wish you'd tell the women! I've had more women tell me they really enjoy taking my penis in their mouth but the idea of swallowing semen or even holding it in their mouth before spitting it out really turns them off, so they usually avoid oral sex. You'd do all us men a big favor if you let them know that we enjoy their mouths on us, it can feel wonderful, but it's definitely not the main pleasure, and not necessary for my sense of closeness and completeness."

"Once in a while."
"Not important at all."
"No, but that's fun, too."
"Not necessarily."

And lots more of the same. In fact, only one man reported that it was necessary and important to his pleasure. Since lots of women do, as the first comment suggests, regard the swallowing of semen as a necessary part of fellatio, and may refrain from performing this sex act because it is distasteful to them, it may add to their freedom of sexual expression to know that men enjoy having their penises orally pleasured with or without ejaculating in the woman's mouth. Note, however, that not one single man said he *didn't like* such ejaculating once in a while. The message to women continues to be, "Do what is giving you pleasure while giving me pleasure."

114. Could you enjoy being in a relationship with a woman who enjoys sex but hates fellatio?

I asked this question because of a lovely woman friend of mine who really hates fellatio, thinks it's "unpleasant and degrading and yucky," to quote her. We have another mutual woman friend, in contrast, who enjoys fellatio. In fact, she is a wonderful artist who creates erotic drawings, often featuring oral sex, and often with herself as the model. The woman who loves fellatio has had lots of exciting sexual adventures in her life, and is now happily married. The woman who hates it has had a great deal of difficulty finding loving men in her life. Not to equate the two, but since the woman who hates fellatio still loves having a man perform oral sex on *her,* she is creating distance and disparity in her sexual relating, saying to the man, "I really like your doing something that I wouldn't do in a million years." Only a certain type of man will respond to this double standard, to this unwillingness on her part to even explore the possibility that this is something she might be able to enjoy. I'm not suggesting that she has to perform fellatio to have a successful relationship, but I am strongly suggesting that she limits her choices by being very rigid on this issue. In order to have freedom of choice, we have to have viable alternatives. Someone who can't do something because of fear, disgust, or discomfort can't freely choose *not* to do it. He or she is being forced not to do it by beliefs, rather than by preferring or choosing not to do it.

Since these are very special men, I expected that they'd be more flexible than most, and they were. Fully 35 percent said they could certainly enjoy such a relationship, and several indicated they now *do* enjoy such a relationship. Eighteen percent answered with emphatic "No!" responses. What intrigued me the most were the rest of the answers, almost half of them, which seemed hesitant and somewhat reluctant:

"Maybe."
"Yes, depending on why she 'hates' that."
"Not sure."
"I could learn to enjoy it."
"Yes, but I'd miss it."
"I could be, but it detracts from our sexual experience."

Remember, these are all men who said they enjoy fellatio immensely and that it's an important part of their sexual pleasure. But they are all also very loving and supportive men who probably wouldn't reject the woman just because she might have difficulty with one aspect of sexuality. This support might be a very loving act, but it could lead to problems later in the relationship. Prostitutes report, for example, that a lot of their business is performing fellatio on men whose wives won't. Perhaps a more clearly thought out answer is the following:

"I really love fellatio, but if I fell in love with an otherwise wonderful and sexually responsive woman, I think I could let go of that need."

115. Do you enjoy cunnilingus as a natural part of your sexual sharing?

"Yes, it excites me to excite her."

"It depends on responsiveness and hygiene."

"Absolutely!"

"It's a super turn-on, particularly if I know she's really enjoying it, it's very, very exciting."

"It's one of my favorite things, but at times it's more like work."

"Sometimes."

"Her reaction to it is important to my pleasure. If she's just lying there and it doesn't seem to be having any effect, forget it. I want feedback, not necessarily verbal, that she's enjoying it. It's exciting when I get lost, beyond the mechanics of just licking, and sort of fusing into her."

"I think early on in my sexual life, I was just doing it to reciprocate for her going down on me, going through the motions because I knew it was something she enjoyed. But in recent years, I just sort of drift off at times and get totally lost in it, like an altered state of consciousness, a total melding, and it's wonderful."

* * *

Three men out of the total group said they did not enjoy cunnilingus at all, all the rest enthusiastically responded in the affirmative, with the exception of about nine men who said they enjoyed it, but it depended on specific conditions.

116. Do you enjoy simultaneous oral sex?

"Sometimes. It can be too intense with both things going on."

"One of the greatest ecstatic moments of my life has been when we have had mutual orgasms in this way."

"As often as possible."

And 90 percent of the rest of the answers were "yes," with the rest being "sometimes." The interesting point here is that several men who said they did not enjoy cunnilingus say they do enjoy simultaneous oral sex. Perhaps having fellatio performed at the same time gives them permission to do something they might otherwise hesitate doing, or maybe the fellatio gives them so much pleasure that they don't notice they're not enjoying the cunnilingus part of it. In any event, among this group, oral sex is here to stay.

117. What other kinds of foreplay turn you on?

"I like contrasts. I enjoy going from humorous play to passion to affection and tenderness and back to ferocious passion."

"Every erogenous zone."

"Touching, rubbing, and stroking each other. Breasts, backs, genitals, etc."

"Genital stroking."

"Full body contact with undulating movement."

"Caressing my legs and thighs very, very softly."

"Passionate sounds and smells."

"Massage, cuddling, showering together."

173

"Having my whole body stroked and played with."
"Licking, gently nibbling, and kissing the entire surface of my body, and my doing the same to her."

118. What qualities and/or skills are your favorite from the woman?

"Good sense of touch. Wonderful, uninhibited sounds from her."
"Good looks, trim bodies, oral sex, multiorgasmic."
"Visible enjoyment of what I was doing."
"French kiss, massage, fellatio . . . supple and passionate during intercourse."
"Seems to love me deeply."
"Passion, gentleness, sensitivity."
"Originality, sensualness, lots of foreplay, stamina, good hip rotation."
"Turned on to me."
"Passionate, orgasmic, and enjoyably open."
"Willing to try new things."
"Each of my favorite sexual partners taught me something new about my own sexual responsiveness. One of my all-time favorites used to love to suck on my toe while I was inside her as we lay on our sides, her back to my front. I was in my mid-thirties and had never even thought of doing this, and it was fantastic!"
"Playfulness, empathetic sensitivity to the point of telepathy, desired total abandon, the ability to receive."

These men certainly know what they've liked.

119. Is there some specific sexual skill in a woman that you like the most?

A very similar question from a slightly different approach.

"They enjoyed foreplay and afterplay, and were willing for us to explore each other's sexuality."

"Good kissing and hugging."
"Very warm, with lots of loving energy, and not really 'mechanical' or gymnastic."
"Tactile empathy. The ability to communicate by touch."
"They were all great cuddlers who loved sleeping next to me."
"The ability to achieve orgasm."
"Oral sex and simultaneous orgasms."

Interestingly, some 30 percent of the men said that their love partners did *not* share any sexual skill or quality in common. This may indicate that they have done a lot of exploring with all types of different sexual partners or that they like variety in the sexual skills different women bring into their lives. Perhaps they simply weren't aware of what it was each of these women had in common.

In working with people on their relationship issues, I always find it fascinating to discover what it is that *all* of the people they've been deeply involved with had in common. There's always something, though not always a sexual skill or quality. Identifying what specific characteristics we seem to choose time and time again can help pinpoint exactly what we want in a relationship partner.

120. Is there a former lover you would like to have sex with again? What was so special?

"Yes. Our bodies just seemed to fit together more perfectly than with any other partner. There was no way we could twist or turn without molding totally to each other's body, and her mouth was wonderfully soft for kissing."

"She was the most beautiful woman I have ever been with, and her sensual nature was a real turn-on. And she wanted nothing more than to give me as much pleasure as possible. If she weren't married now with two children, I'd definitely want to make love with her. We still keep in touch, and somewhere below the surface —with my current happy relationship and all—I have this hope that she might someday once again be available to me."

"If I weren't involved currently, there are some I would consider. Some are better than others, but all are different. Each has her own unique specialness."

"Yes, she was a close friend I enjoyed being with."

"Yes, a great satisfier."

"Yes, really ecstatic orgasms."

"Such powerful orgasms that I seriously worried about being thrown out of bed. They were scary and unforgettable."

"Yes—good sounds, movement, and enjoyment."

"Nothing surpasses the excitement and depth I have with my wife, but I did know a girl once who could play a man's nervous system like a violin."

"Yes, my love for her is what made it great."

"One woman came immediately to mind, but I recently got to stay with her in her new house in another city, and there was just no interest on either of our parts. We did feel a lot of special love energy, but no sexual energy.

"Yes. The spontaneity and lack of long-term demands."

"Oh, yes! We never had to discuss whether to make love, or check out each other's mood. If we were awake and in bed, we both wanted it, and it was very freeing and as close to sexual nirvana as I've ever been on a consistent basis. We've since both gone on to other relationships, more satisfying relationships in other respects, but are still friends and have told each other that we have never found a better lover in the six years apart. I think she would love to have sex with me again, but her current live-in lover could never handle it."

"Yes, and not because there was anything so special, but because we never seemed to be sexually compatible. I have since expanded my sexual experience and sensitivity, and I would like to see if it could be different with her now."

"Yes. She prided herself on providing me with wonderful, ecstatic sex, and there was one fantastic position where I sat on a chair facing the end of the bed, and she sat on the bed and slowly slid down onto my lap, using the bed to push herself against me.

. . . I'm not even sure I could tell another woman how to duplicate it, and I wouldn't want to dent my great erotic memories."

"One lady who lived in another city and whom I got to see only every few months. She had the wildest sense of adventure, doing such crazy things as unzipping me in an elevator; making love on top of the coats on a bed at a friend's house we were visiting, never knowing who was going to walk in, scaring the daylights out of me; even once doing it in the back of a car as friends were driving us to a resort where we were both going to meet our primary partners, pulling up into the parking lot where they were both waiting for us, and trying not to look as if we had just had sex. It was crazy and nerve-racking, but I've never been as spontaneous with anyone else. This was five years ago, and I met her last year and even spent a day at the beach with her, and all the sexual attraction seemed to be gone on both sides, but I'd give anything to get back together with her the way she was."

"Yes, definitely, my ex-wife. We could never live together again, but she was great in bed."

These men don't have fantasy images of their ideal woman, but they definitely have fond sexual memories and warm feelings for former partners.

There's something very romantic about remembering a former lover and one's earlier years. I recently had the opportunity to visit a city where I had known a very warm woman in my presexual youth. It had been eighteen years since we were together, and we spent a quiet evening, with her preparing a candlelit gourmet dinner. It was innocent, as it had been then. Her beauty had not diminished, and the touch of her ultrasoft lips in a goodnight kiss vividly brought back memories of a night we had spent necking so many years ago. No one has ever kissed me exactly as she did. The fact that no two people touch or caress or make love exactly alike may well be what nurtures our fond memories. Each partner we encounter touches a different part of us in a different way. When a relationship ends, sometimes that part goes into hibernation, only to be reawakened by an occasional memory.

Several of the men reported that what was so special in their former lovers was the quality and/or intensity of their orgasms. Let's look at this facet of what men want sexually from women.

121. Do you feel guilty or responsible if your partner has difficulty achieving orgasm?

"Most of the time I think I would . . . and have . . . although at times, if she's really the right person, it's not such a big deal."

"Women keep talking about being responsible for their own orgasms, but I still get the feeling that she's blaming me if she has a hard time climaxing."

"Well, yes . . . even though my mind says otherwise."

"I like a woman who has orgasms easily. I don't like having to feel like it's a chore, that I have to work hard to satisfy them."

"No. As long as she has an orgasm most of the time, I don't have any problems with guilt or responsibility."

"No, definitely not. I just do the best I can to please her."

"It depends. She may think it's my job to make her climax. I lived with one woman for four years who never had an orgasm during sex with me . . . had never had one with a man. The only way she could come was to masturbate. It was about a year before she felt O.K. about masturbating with me present, after we had made love. She loved sex and me inside her, but just couldn't come that way, and never laid blame on me. She really taught me that women are *in charge of their own pleasure."*

Even these emotionally mature and stable men admit that they occasionally feel guilty or uncomfortable when a woman has difficulty having an orgasm. (Only about 20 percent of the men said they don't ever feel guilty or responsible in this situation.) They don't like this, and I would imagine that a woman who takes responsibility for her own orgasms would be the most satisfying to them.

One of the problems in male-female relating is that we often assume the other person should know what's going on in our minds and bodies without our having to tell them. All the research studies that show most relationships and marriage break up because of poor communication are really saying the problem is that men and women don't tell each other what is going on, in sex or other aspects of their relationships.

122. Do you think you always know when a woman has an orgasm, or do you want her to give you some kind of information on this?

"I need some information."

"I feel dumb that I don't know. Sometimes when I'm with a new woman I have difficulty knowing whether she's had an orgasm or not. And it's very hard for me to ask that question, you know—'By the way, have you come yet? Are you coming now? Was that an orgasm?'"

"I'm a little embarrassed about asking whether she's had an orgasm . . . maybe she'll answer, 'No, you're not even close . . . you're terrible!'"

"No, sometimes orgasms are very passive in women, and it's hard to tell. I would usually ask if she did, so I know if I am handling her properly."

"I know when my wife has one."

"I want some information on what's happening for her."

"I prefer that she be very verbal. She doesn't necessarily have to be a screamer, just so you know that what you're doing really feels great, and she's open enough to let you know that you're driving her out of her mind, giving her a lot of pleasure."

"No, information is appreciated."

"No, I don't always know, and I'd like her to tell me."

"Her orgasms are her business, not mine. I'm just going to give her as much love as possible."

"I want her to tell me. It's certainly better than a very silent woman who might have had fourteen orgasms and you'd have no idea, because not only is she so silent, but her body never twitches. She doesn't have to be a screaming, writhing animal, but it's nice to know what's going on with her."

Pretty conclusively, the men want information from the woman, verbal or nonverbal.

123. Do you prefer the woman to have many orgasms, or just one or two?

"Before being with women who are multiorgasmic, I would have said I'd like to be with a woman I can have sex with and we climax together once and that's it. And I think part of my reasoning was that I would have felt safe with that. Now, I wouldn't be satisfied with that, because I've gotten into a much more intense, passionate sexuality."

"I prefer quality, not quantity."

"Yes, many orgasms."

"It doesn't matter."

"As many as possible."

"For me, it's not the number of orgasms, it's the kind of contact that we're making. One of my most beautiful moments sexually was just lying gazing in her eyes and hardly moving, just being in total oneness. Sometimes I actually see orgasms getting in the way. My ex-wife would be preoccupied with her trying to get an orgasm rather than [involved in it together] with me."

"The number doesn't matter, but I like a woman who orgasms easily. I don't like having to feel like it's a chore, that I have to work hard to satisfy them."

"The main thing is how loving we are together, but if everything else is O.K., I enjoy having her go crazy with multiple orgasms."

"As long as she has that wonderful contented smile on her face, I don't care how many orgasms she has."

More than half the men expressed a preference for multiple orgasms, which was unexpected information for me. Of course, some of these men do attract more sexually experienced women, and these women are more likely to have more than one orgasm. I also found it interesting that the remainder of the men did not state that they prefer one or two orgasms, merely that they had no preference at all. This may mean that men who have experienced multiorgasmic women tend to prefer this kind of response, while those who haven't just don't think it's important.

I checked with a small sampling of men who had responded in both ways and found that those who had no strong preference did not have strong, committed relationships with multiorgasmic women. Those who preferred many orgasms were either in, or had been in, satisfying primary love relationships with multiorgasmic women. This was just a sampling, however. What does seem evident in these answers, and in additional conversation I've had with these men, is a desire to have women come into their lives already fully developed sexually. Men like women who have powerful sexual responses, who have sensitized their own bodies so that they can easily get excited and easily climax. Men want women to have a good time sexually.

One problem here is that our culture has almost made a cult of the orgasm—consider, for example, the ridiculous debates between those who advocate clitoral orgasms versus vaginal orgasms, multiple orgasms versus single orgasms, etc. As I wrote in my book *Transcendental Sex* (Holt, Rinehart and Winston, 1978), "Orgasm is a total body experience, involving increased respiration and heart rate, muscular tension, urethral and anal contractions, and a change in brain wave patterns. The important factor here, however, is that it is the subjective experience that determines how good sex is for you, not how many orgasms you have. Your one orgasm may be more satisfying for you than someone else's half dozen. When you reduce sexual performance to a statistical orgasm count, you remove all of the love and caring and flow."

One of the ways in which women inform men as to their sexual satisfaction is by the spontaneous sounds they make during lovemaking.

124. What kinds of sounds do you enjoy hearing from the woman while making love?
"All kinds, as long as they are expressive of what is going on."
"Moans, sighs, giggles, screams, anything."
"Any sounds. Grunts and groans are good. I don't like quiet sex."
"Any and all."
"Any natural sounds."
"Oohs and ahhs."
"Moans, words of pleasure, yells."
"Having her scream out my name amidst her passionate moans is great."
"Sighing, cooing . . . no screaming."
"Everything. But if she's screaming, I don't want her to yell out my name so it's heard right through the walls."
"Any indication that she's enjoying the experience."

Men like women to make sounds of appreciation and pleasure, but do they necessarily want them to talk about what they want *while* involved in sex?

125. What is your response when the woman talks about what she wants *while* you are making love?
"Fine with me . . . doesn't mean I'll do it."

"I usually do it."

"The director type drives me up the wall. You know, 'Put your finger there; no, no, up higher.' It's like being in wood shop or listening to my drill sergeant in the army."

"I like a woman to be verbal—sort of a mutual discussion as we go along as to what feels nice. There have also been times when she talked openly about sex when it's made me feel uncomfortable. And sometimes after sex, if I verbally share how great it was and she's silent, I feel uncomfortable, like maybe it wasn't great for her."

"If she's tactful and honest, fine."

"As long as she does it appropriately."

"Mostly a no-no. Sometimes good."

"I enjoy knowing what she wants me to do."

"It all depends on how she does it. If she says something like, 'Ooh, that feels good, please do that some more,' I love giving her what she wants. But if she starts giving orders and instructions like a gym teacher, forget it."

"Usually good. Sometimes it distracts and feels like orders."

"Great, if she is receptive and appreciative rather than demanding."

"I love it if it's something I enjoy doing for her. If not, I may feel pressured or guilty if I don't do it."

"If it's just, 'lower, harder, softer, more, feels good,' that's O.K. But no long harangues, please!"

"I appreciate it and do what I can to comply. I get bothered when all she talks about is what she doesn't want."

"I tend to react initially somewhat negatively . . . but if her tone and actions let me know it isn't some kind of putdown or personal criticism, then I can usually enjoy the suggestion."

"The one instruction that really turns me off is when I'm asked to talk while making love. I like to concentrate on the physical sensations, and talk is distracting, though I can shut it out if she is talking too much."

"I'd rather she tell me what she wants before or after, not during."

* * *

These men don't seem to mind women asking for what they want during lovemaking, as long as they do it with tenderness and without a demanding tone or attitude. Only about 10 percent actually said they don't like it when the woman talks about what she wants them to do.

126. **Is there anything the woman could ask you for sexually that you really don't want to give or do?**

"Anal intercourse; the idea of it just turns me off, so I usually don't see them anymore, or just avoid talking about it."

"I've had a few that at first I was uncomfortable with, like a suggestion that I masturbate in front of her."

"I have an extremely short tongue."

"Sometimes I don't want to perform cunnilingus."

"If I was asked to give anal sex, I wouldn't."

"No, not really."

"Not a thing."

"Not so far."

"Sometimes during fellatio it feels wonderful, and she says, 'Now I want you to put it in me.' I really don't want to stop what is happening, but I usually do because I feel selfish or self-indulgent if I don't give her what she wants. Once I'm inside her, it's fine."

Slightly more than half the men said there wasn't anything they've been asked for that they didn't want to give or do. Are men assertive in asking women for what *they* want sexually?

127. **Is there anything you are embarrassed to ask a woman to do for you sexually?**

"No, my desires are simple and uncomplicated."

"I usually have trouble asking for anything specific."

184

"No."

"Not if we are involved in a relationship."

"Sometimes I'm embarrassed, but I ask anyway."

"Sometimes I have difficulty asking a woman to give fellatio."

"I tend to hint rather than ask."

"I don't think so. Possibly to make love while she's having her period."

"Nothing anymore, except maybe bringing another woman into our sexual activity."

"Sometimes it's awkward for me to ask someone to caress me while I'm caressing her. Sometimes it's just a feeling of, 'I wish she knew this and I didn't have to say anything.'"

Just about half the men said there was nothing they were embarrassed to ask for, again indicating that this is a pretty open group, comfortable with their own sexuality and good at communicating what they want.

Women tell me men tend to avoid discussing birth control—who's responsible for it, asking the woman whether she's taken care of it. So I asked the following question.

128. **When about to engage in sexual activity with a new lover, do you bring up the issue of birth control, do you want the woman to mention it, or do you prefer that she just take care of it without saying a word?**

"I usually bring it up—actually it got so it wasn't a big deal, especially since it's usually appreciated."

"I usually ask about it."

"I always bring it up, though I don't want to, but the consequences are too great if I make a mistake."

"I prefer she just take care of it."

"Sometime I'll bring it up, but if I think she's experienced, I just assume she's either taken care of it or will say something to me."

"I always let her know ahead of time that I've had a vasectomy."

"I've become more comfortable asking if I need protection."

"I used to be very uncomfortable about this, and it's been one of the big pluses of having my vasectomy to get it over with easily."

"Since a lot of women have so many problems with the pill and IUDs, I usually ask."

"My experience has been that the woman almost always brings it up first, quite naturally telling me what kind of protection she is using. If not, I bring it up, but I prefer that she take care of it."

"I always wanted to but usually didn't bring it up, then I felt guilty about it and brought it up sometime during our lovemaking. Since I got 'fixed,' the big change is no guilt about having to ask."

"After having been involved with the harshness of abortion, I definitely bring it up myself!"

"I don't like being in a situation where I have to ask, but I will if there's no indication she has taken care of it."

"My first choice is that she's had her tubes tied. My second is that she has taken care of it in some other way. My third is that she bring it up. And that I have to bring it up or take care of it is definitely my last choice."

Half of even this group of sensitive, caring men want the woman to just take care of it, though about one-third did say that they will bring it up if the woman doesn't. Fifteen percent have completely taken care of this issue with vasectomies.

129. What is your very favorite sexual position?

"Male dominant."

"Female on top."

"I love entering her from the rear when we are lying in a side-to-side, spooning position."

186

"I like to enter her from the rear while she is lying on her stomach, sometimes lifting her pelvis toward me with a pillow under her."

"Varies with the partner, but generally it's me on top with my legs astride hers."

"The good old missionary position."

"Woman on top."

"Her on top. That way I can hold off longer without climaxing."

"Her on top facing away from me and lifting herself up and down."

"Constantly in motion, moving around and switching off. Side-by-side is nice for resting. I also like seated, with her astride. Come to think of it, I haven't found any that I don't like."

No dramatic new trends here, although there is a strong indication that the woman-on-top position has replaced the missionary as the favorite of most men.

130. What do you most enjoy having happen immediately following intercourse?

"Just cuddle and smile at each other."

"Cuddling."

"Some quiet time, or else some quiet talk and cuddling."

"Snuggling, kissing, and spooning."

"Closeness, relaxing, talking, sharing our feelings."

"Hold each other."

"A kiss and then rest."

"Gentle caressing."

"Talking."

Only one man said he wants to go right to sleep by himself after sex, a traditional behavior pattern many women have complained about. Women have also complained that men want to break the flow by getting up and going home after sex, instead of spending the night (if they are not living with the woman). *These* men seem to enjoy sleeping with a woman.

131. Do you enjoy sleeping cuddled next to the woman?

"It's one of my very favorite things to do in all the world."
"Yes, but not engulfed by her."
"I enjoy it, but I can't do it. I sleep light, and we roll into each other too much."
"Is there any other way?"

Not much ambiguity here. Again, the more sensitized and aware a man becomes, the more any relating to a woman becomes a total physical connection, not just genital contact. Sleeping together, cuddled up, usually provides as much or more physical contact than intercourse. It fulfills many of our touch needs in a completely satisfying way.

132. What is the difference in your feelings toward the woman after lovemaking?

A lot of women believe that men will pull back from intimacy "after they've gotten what they want from you," as the old wives' tale goes. I asked a group of men described in glowing terms by the women they know this question and the following one to ascertain their true feelings in this situation.

"I feel as though we've shared something special and there'll always be a bond."
"I feel closer after we've made love—no more barriers or games to play."
"My feelings grow deeper."
"I don't think I can generalize. Sometimes I'm less clear about

the meaning of the relationship when I am sexually involved."

"I think a part of me holds back being totally open to a woman when I don't know whether we will feel good together sexually, especially if I am sexually attracted to her. After sex, assuming it feels good and right, I let much more of myself be exposed to her. And maybe because of this, I tend to wait as long as possible before having sex—getting to know her, touch her, kiss and caress her before I am ready for the vulnerability that comes after making love."

"A feeling of closeness and mutual sharing."

"I feel closer after, because you learn more about each other during sex."

"Closer after sex."

"Usually the relationship reaches a more intimate level after making love."

"Closer."

This is another area in which these men unanimously agree, or at least 96 percent of them do. Four or five of them don't seem too sure and think it varies with the partner. I also found it fascinating that 85 percent of the answers included the word *closer* or *closeness*. Since a lot of women believe that men shy away from feelings of closeness, this should be heartening news for them.

133. Once you've had sex with a woman, do you find her more or less desirable and exciting?

We covered the issue of closeness. What about sexual desire? Is it true that a lot of the excitement is contained in the uncertainty, in not knowing whether your partner will have sex with you, in not knowing whether it will feel good? Does desire disappear with the mystery?

"No change."

"More desirable."

"It depends. Sometimes after sex I'll realize that all we had going for us was sexual desire, and once that's realized, I lose interest. But if she's someone I am really excited about being with on all levels, then I find her even more desirable once we've had a mutually satisfying sexual encounter."

"Generally more. As you get to know one another you have a better idea of how to please."

"More, because there's the excitement of getting to know her body even better once you've gotten off to a good sexual start. And it does get better as you get more relaxed and knowledgeable with each other."

"It depends on whether she's a sexual partner I see once in a while, in which case the excitement builds, or someone I am getting deeply emotionally involved or committed with, which may mean that my fears of intimacy get in the way of sexual desire, and it seems to diminish."

"More. More. More. More. More."

"Depends on my reaction. If the sex was good, she is more exciting. If it was just O.K., I find her less attractive."

"More by far."

"That depends on other elements of the relationship. Generally more for a while, then thing gets a little routine."

"I must confess that sometimes I start taking her for granted, unless she keeps me guessing by not being totally available; then this keeps my interest up. I wish this weren't so, but that's the way it is."

"Probably more, if she's a good lover."

This time 90 percent of the men said they would find her more desirable.

Another complaint a lot of women have shared with me is that men don't seem to enjoy kissing as much as *they* do, and once the relationship has progressed from kissing to sexual intimacy, the kissing usually dramatically diminishes.

134. Once you are in a sexual relationship with a woman, is kissing her a lot still an important part of your pleasure?

"Yup."

"Very definitely."

"I assume you mean kissing her on the lips, and yes it is, but now I have lots more places to kiss as well."

"It tends to be important, but not as important during sex as it was when we started the relationship."

"Absolutely. We ought to encourage post-marital kissing."

"If she's a really good kisser, yes. If not, then I tend to avoid kissing."

Another near unanimous response.

As men come to see intimacy as a total sharing on many more levels than just the physical, they also tend to become more free in their physical contacts. They get less caught up in preset patterns of relating. Prominent among these is the progressive buildup followed by letdown— being attracted to a woman, staring to know her, holding hands, kissing, petting, sexual intimacy, followed by loss of interest. This sequence has really deprived a lot of men of the pleasures of true intimacy.

At the beginning, even sexual relating is superficial. A lot of men and women have carried on a whole series of superficial relationships, never allowing them to get deeper. The boredom they often experience is a symptom of their subconscious fear of deeper intimacy and commitment. The sense of "oneness" that some men describe feeling with a woman never comes at the beginning. It takes time to build in order to trust and then let go. When we block ourselves off by running away either physically or emotionally after sexual intimacy has begun, we miss the chance to discover how much love we can really receive, how good more total involvement with another person can be.

The men of this survey are obviously not looking for sexual pleasure as a final goal in relating to a woman. Rather, they see sex as a way of expressing something more, one of several ways in which men and women can enjoy each other. Though certainly not completely free of sexual limitations and hangups, these men are freer than most, and definitely more sensitive to their partners' needs and wants. Whether this is a result of the sexual revolution, their own personal growth, or the fact that women are asking for more of what they want from a man is anybody's guess—probably a combination of all three. In any event, it *is* making for more relaxed and more satisfying sexual relationships.

As I wrote in *Transcendental Sex* six years ago, "Sexual energy is merely a manifestation of our basic life energy, and as such is most fully appreciated as a part of the totality of our being. If the only time you feel awake and alive is during sexual activity, then you may be missing the point. If you are dull, lethargic, and uninterested in life, you're not going to be a very sensitive or exciting lover. With a strong sense of vitality, you will have an abundance of energy to share with your love partner."

These men do seem to have an abundance of vitality, and they want women with that same sense of aliveness. In the final analysis, what's the point of being with another person if that person is not bringing more life into your life?

6

SOME MALE
CONCLUSIONS

What we have so far is a bunch of men wanting a bunch of things from a bunch of women. Let's see if we can sort it out some more—clarify what men really want by drawing some conclusions based on the majority of responses. Then, at the end of this chapter, we'll consider two final questions.

Remember, I am drawing conclusions from looking at the same responses you've looked at in the preceding chapters. You may draw your own conclusions.

Not every man interviewed would necessarily agree with the following statements, but most would. The men were chosen from every geographical area across the country. They range in age from twenty-eight to sixty-seven, most of them being in their thirties and forties. I am also assuming that *most* men considered by women to be loving, sensitive, open, and vulnerable *would* agree with these statements. You may find it interesting to gather such a group of men together and check this out with them.

1. **A man is most likely to ask a woman out who shows an interest in him, is physically appealing, and with whom he feels comfortable.**
Men are encouraged to ask women out when they feel good being with them. Nothing makes a man feel better than the woman letting him know she enjoys his company, at the same time looking good and creating a comfortable atmosphere.

2. **A woman does not have to look like a movie star to attract a man, but her chances are much better if she is not overweight.**
For whatever reason, a trim figure is an absolute prerequisite for most men.

3. **Most men prefer attractive long hair to attractive short hair in a woman.**

4. **Most men still prefer women in dresses rather than slacks or jeans.**

5. **Most men are turned off by excessive use of perfume and makeup.**

6. **These men most often find women they are attracted to in places where people with interests similar to theirs meet.**

Most of the warm and loving men that women say they are looking for are not to be found at bars, in singles clubs, or through computer dating services.

7. A man is most likely to fall in love with and enter a committed relationship with a woman who lets him know at the beginning exactly how she feels about him.

These men are sometimes intrigued by a woman of mystery, but they certainly don't want to live with her or marry her.

8. A man prefers doing something on a first date that gives him a chance to get to know the woman.

Movies and other forms of spectator entertainment are not preferred for a first date.

9. Men would much rather go to a romantic restaurant for a first date than have the woman cook for them.

10. A man wants a woman to touch him carefully and tenderly when just getting to know her.

11. Sensitive men like women to talk about sex on a first date, but not aggressively.

12. Most men do not want a woman to come on too strong in a sexual way when they first meet her.

These men sometimes feel that a sexually aggressive woman may demand too much from them performance-wise.

13. Most of these men do not want or need to have sex on a first date. They prefer a buildup of trust and intimacy, which usually takes a little longer.

14. Men are most likely to be turned off on a first date by a woman who is boring, not interested in them personally, or cold and distant.

15. Men want the unconditional love they got from their mothers, but without the critical, nagging, domineering parental behavior.

16. After getting what they've always fantasized about in a woman, a lot of men realize they really don't want it.

This runs the gamut from a great body to sexual abandon to a certain age or hairstyle.

17. Most men have fallen in love with "potential" and later regretted it.

18. These men are getting more of what they want from women than they did a few years ago.

19. Men want women to bring tenderness, gregariousness, and emotional honesty into a relationship, to offset any deficiencies they have in these areas.

20. These men have learned a lot about loving from the women in their lives.

21. A loving man wants to love a woman who is an interesting conversationalist.

22. Most men enjoy spending evenings and weekends with the women in their lives. Most also resent spending more time with a woman than they

would choose to, just because the woman wants them to.

23. There's not much a man wants a woman to give up when she enters a relationship with him, except other men as sexual partners.

24. Sex is one of the main things men want from a woman they want to be with.

25. These men don't do a lot of fantasizing about their "ideal" woman.

26. Other than sex, most men want companionship, friendship, and someone to listen to them in a relationship.

27. Most men prefer a woman they can just enjoy being with, as opposed to going out and doing lots of things together.

28. Men like being surprised by women.

29. When they do or give something nice, men want a woman to respond with appreciation and enthusiasm.

30. Men thoroughly enjoy getting compliments from women, but they don't always get as many or the kind they want.

31. Men like the feeling of being with an attractive woman in public.

32. Men are threatened by "pushy," overly aggressive women.

33. Men are threatened by sexual demands and commitment demands.

These men want to make their own decisions about when they're ready for more intimacy and a deeper commitment.

34. Most men are occasionally intimidated by an exceptionally beautiful woman.

35. Most men are repulsed by a woman whose lifestyle reflects confusion or uncertainty, but not by a woman who is uncertain due to being at a temporary crossroads in her life.

36. These men want more clear statements from women, less ambiguity.

37. Most men are at least somewhat confused about their own role in a relationship today.

38. Most men have at least one thing they would be uncomfortable telling a woman.

39. Most men have some fear of intimacy. They may withdraw if the woman comes on too strong, demanding too much commitment before they're ready for it.

40. Men don't want women to see their opening up and sharing more feelings as necessarily a desire for a deeper relationship commitment.

41. Men feel most comfortable opening up and showing their tender side when the woman treats them gently, which includes having a gentle touch.

42. Men are easily hurt by women who put them down sexually, attack and criticize them, or express unprovoked anger toward them.

43. Lots of emotional turmoil in a woman can frighten a man away.

44. Men like their women to be emotionally stable and easygoing.

45. Men will avoid discussing some things even in happy love relationships.

46. Men want to choose the time and place to discuss serious relationship issues.

47. Men find it most difficult to ask a woman for sex, for time alone, and that she pay her own way.

48. Men find it most difficult to give a woman time, attention, commitment, and to share more of their feelings.

49. Men believe women are more aware of and better at expressing their feelings.

50. Sensitive, loving men prefer that a woman be liberated and independent.

51. Most of the men believe the women's movement has made women more desirable.

52. Most of these men want the woman to offer to pay her share of a restaurant bill.

53. These men feel very comfortable being with a woman who earns as much as or more than they do.

54. Most of the men want a woman with a career they can respect.

55. Men love to cuddle and be massaged.

56. These men have women friends in their lives.

57. The men would rather be with a woman friend than a woman who just offers them sexual release.

58. Men love to have their genitals caressed and stroked, even without anything else sexual happening.

59. Men like to touch and be touched in public, but in a gentle, dignified way. They don't like kissing or blatant sexual touching in public.

60. Before sexual activity, what turns men on the most is for the woman to let the man know she is excited by him.

61. Men want sexually open and responsive women, but want them also to be gentle and sensitive to their needs.

62. Men want women to let them know when they are in the mood for lovemaking.

63. These men want women who are sexually experienced and skillful.

64. Most men consider fellatio important to their sexual pleasure with a woman.

65. It is not important for their pleasure that they ejaculate in her mouth.

66. Most of the men enjoy cunnilingus.

67. Most of the men enjoy simultaneous oral sex.

68. Most of these men have former lovers they would like to have sex with again.

69. Most of the men sometimes feel guilty or responsible if a woman doesn't have an orgasm.

70. The men want the woman to let them know, verbally or nonverbally, when she has an orgasm.

71. More and more men are seeking woman who can have multiple orgasms.

72. Men like women to make sounds of appreciation and pleasure during sex.

73. Men can enjoy a woman asking for what she wants during sex, but not if she's demanding.

74. For most men, the favorite sexual position is the woman sitting on top.

75. These men enjoy being close and sleeping with a woman after sex.

76. These men feel closer to a woman after having

sex with her and find her even more desirable then.

77. Even after having progressed to sexual intimacy with a woman, these men really enjoy kissing.

These seventy-seven statements do not cover all the questions asked of this group of men—some of the answers were not uniformly conclusive. One of the surprising things for me in gathering this information was how much consensus there actually was among these men.

If I had to make a blanket statement about what sensitive, loving men really want from women, I would have to say:

An attractive, slender, long-haired woman, in a challenging career, who is sexually responsive and talented but not threatening; who will treat him tenderly, is a good listener, has interesting things to say, is good at touching, massage, and oral sex; who likes to cuddle, thinks he's terrific and lets him know it, does not press for a commitment until he's ready, has multiple orgasms with moans; who pays her own way, has self-confidence, can surprise him, and is never "pushy."

This doesn't cover every detail, but most of the men I interviewed—and I myself—would be quite happy with this combination or with any woman who had most of these qualities.

And though you may now think we have asked these men just about everything there is to ask about what they want from women, there are two more questions. Totally different in nature, each has something to do with what men want to tell women.

135. **If you could be totally honest with a woman you are involved with—without fear of incurring her disapproval or harming the relationship in any way—what one thing would you say to her?**

"I love you sexually only and for no other reason. And that is the only basis on which I will continue our relationship."

"Inundate me with more and more love!"

"I find you sexually attractive; I don't like your inability to bend with the way things happen instead of the way you want them to go."

"Be your own person. Don't be needy or dependent on me."

"If you can't share and you don't grow and keep trying to grow as I do, then I can't be in a relationship with you."

"I don't really mind the fact that you have one breast, but I wish you wouldn't insist on coming to bed nude instead of in a nice negligee. One breast is fine, but I really don't find that red, scarred area very attractive, and I think you are constantly looking for proof that I still love you. It's getting very tiresome."

"I don't want children, I've never wanted children, and you turn me off every time you start harping on the subject, when you know exactly how I feel."

"I wish you wouldn't come on to me when you can see I'm preoccupied or tired. There are times I'm just not in the mood for sex, and times I just go through the motions because I don't want to disappoint you."

"I can't stand your brother and his wife and kids. I hate it every time we go visit them, and I wish you would just go alone."

"That marriage can take many forms of shared energy and time and that if two people could be open, some surprising alternatives could result. Preconceptions are what get in the way of beautiful new realities."

"I would love to make love to you and your sister in the same bed, one after the other."

"I want you to be more loving."

"Your cooking stinks."

"When we were just dating, your brother's wife came over to my place one afternoon . . . and we carried on a two-month affair. She begged me not to ever tell you, and I guess you couldn't handle it, but I feel it creates a barrier between us."

"I would like an occasional weekend off from seeing you."

"During sex, when you start breathing very deeply, your breath really turns me off from all the cigarette smell coming up."

"I would tell her I love her, and that saying that doesn't mean I want to be with her exclusively or forever."

"Though it sometimes excites me, your telling me about your swinging sex life keeps me from wanting to see you more. I'm really concerned about your catching something and giving it to me."

"I would say, 'I love you, but you are not as good a lover as my ex-wife, and I would love to be able to see her once in a while just for sex.'"

"That I'm afraid she's going to leave me."

"I owe my ex-girlfriend ten thousand dollars and I'm paying her back a little at a time, which is why I sometimes seem to hesitate before spending money on you."

"I'm sick of Sunday dinners at your folks' house, with the same people, the same conversation, and the same damn overdone chicken . . . even the same comments about watching 60 Minutes!"

"Your spiritual master bores me stiff, and I think you're less spiritual than you were before you started going to his meetings."

"You have terrible taste in clothes, and I wish I could afford to hire someone to dress you right."

"I love your kids, and I wish you hadn't given up custody of them to your ex-husband, because I'd love to have them live with us."

"You hurt my feelings when you take out your vibrator and masturbate if I tell you I'm not in the mood for sex or am busy. I wish you'd wait for me, or do it in private."

"I want you to stay in bed in the morning and love me instead of hopping up to go for a run or do your exercises or cook breakfast."

Wow! A lot of stuff there, and a lot of secrets. I found these answers fascinating, sometimes sad, and indicative of the fact that we all have a long way to go before reaching total honesty in a relationship. About 20 percent of the men didn't answer this one, and many of the answers that I didn't use were similar to those quoted.

I think it would be wonderful if we could look our partner in the eye and suggest that we each tell the other something we've been afraid to tell up to now, because we've been afraid they would be hurt, feel misunderstand, or become angry—perhaps a five-minute period in which we promise that no matter what is said, we would hear it with love and acceptance and the knowledge that none of us is perfect. Wouldn't it be nice if our desire to communicate some of these darker events or desires or opinions were seen as a desire to share ourselves totally with this other person, far overshadowing any negative material contained in what we actually say? I can't think of anyone I've ever been with to whom I've really told it *all.* How about you?

And, finally:

136. Finish this sentence: *"All things considered, women are_____"*

"Beautiful."

"Wonderful."

"People in interesting bodies."

"More fun to be with than men."

"The mirror of men."
"Unlivable-withoutable!"
"All there is worth living for."
"Wonder-full."
"The best of all things considered."
"So much more than we ever give them credit for."
"All that makes life interesting, loving, confusing, and satisfying."
"Much more fun to sleep with than myself."

Though interesting and sometimes facetious, these answers are not really a complete portrayal of the feelings of most of the men. In order to show you that, I would have had to repeat the word "wonderful" over and over again, with an occasional "great" thrown in. Half the men responded with "wonderful."

In closing, what can we 101 men say about women? We've told you lots of things we want from them, and lots of things we get from them. Perhaps we can also tell you how much we love them, and how little of what we really want we would be getting without them in our lives!

APPENDIX

THE
LOVE PARTNER
QUESTIONNAIRE

Now that you've found how much more you can learn about another person by asking the right question, I want to share with you a valuable interpersonal tool from my first book, *My Needs, Your Needs, Our Needs* (Doubleday, 1974). Many couples have reported back over the years that this has had a very powerful positive effect on their relationship, helping them reveal to each other many thoughts, feelings, and memories that otherwise might go unshared.

This is not a quiz; there are no winners or losers, just two people getting to know each other better. Many of the obstacles to happy relating are due to a simple lack of information. As this book attempts to fill in a lot of the gaps on what men really want from women, so this list of one hundred questions can fill in a lot of the unknown and unsaid areas of a love relationship. When we don't know something about someone, we tend to fill in the vacuum with assumptions, fantasies, and unrealistic expectations. During the initial stages of any relationship, we can get so involved in the exciting fantasy that we fail to ask some very basic questions.

The one hundred questions here are designed to provide you with lots of useful information about your love partner, about yourself, and about the relationship. These range from very simple "who" and "why" and "what" questions to ones involving some deep feelings. The questions start out with facts and memories and then go on to feelings. Don't feel forced to answer/ask all of them at once. Choose the pace best suited for the two of you. One suggested format:

1. Start with ten questions.
2. You ask one question, your partner answers.
3. Your partner asks you the same question, and you answer.
4. You both share any feelings you have about this question.
5. After asking and answering ten questions, decide whether you both would prefer continuing at this time.

Avoid passing judgment on your partner as you learn these new things about him or her. Avoid telling your partner what you think a proper or "right" answer should be.

You can vary the environment for this interpersonal exercise. You can face each other, making eye contact. You can hold hands. You might even try asking and answering these questions while lying in each other's arms.

Choose a physical format you both find comfortable and relaxing.

After going through the entire list, you might invent some of your own questions. See if you each can come up with five more questions that might provide you with more useful information about each other.

If you have any difficulty answering any of the questions at this time, go back to them at a later date. A growing relationship reaches new levels of comfort as it builds momentum, and it's important not to force one another to "open up" before it happens easily and naturally. You might also share with each other which answers surprised you the most, which provided information you did not know or even suspect.

And again, as in using the survey questions from this book, remember that love is trusting, not testing. You are trying to know your partner better and letting your partner know you better. Your attitude in sharing this process should be reflective of the kind of loving support you want from someone you love—from someone who loves you. We all want love, and any relationship exploration that doesn't facilitate this isn't worth doing.

1. What kind of a child were you?
2. Describe yourself as you think an adult stranger would have after spending an hour with you at the age of seven or eight.
3. How would your parents have described you as a child?
4. What characteristics did you have as a child that have remained?
5. What characteristics have you lost or changed on reaching adulthood?
6. What was your favorite toy as a child?
7. What is your favorite toy now?

8. What were you most proud of as a child?
9. What event or circumstance of your childhood do you think had the most impact on who you are right now?
10. What was your childhood nickname and how did you feel about it?
11. Do you like your first name now? If not, what would you like instead?
12. What is your favorite color? Can you think of a favorite object that color?
13. What is your favorite possession?
14. Can you name a favorite possession that you no longer possess, and describe your feelings at no longer having it?
15. What is the funniest thing you have ever done as measured by the reaction of your audience at the time?
16. What is the funniest thing that ever happened to you?
17. What is the silliest thing you have ever done?
18. What is the stupidest thing you have ever done?
19. What is your all-time favorite movie? Why does it have special meaning?
20. What is your favorite book? What in it has personal meaning for you?
21. What product, entertainment, or activity that hasn't been available in recent years do you miss most?
22. What fictional hero do you most closely identify with?
23. If you had a choice, would you rather vacation at the seashore, camp in the mountains, or take a luxury cruise? Why?
24. How loving a person are you? If you find it easier, rate yourself on a scale of 1 to 10, with 10 as the most loving. Give an example of something that you think shows how loving you are.